The Acme of All Brocades

Nanjing Yunjin Brocade and Silk-weaving Archives Picture Album

南京云锦及丝织业档案图典

南京市档案馆　编

南京出版传媒集团　南京出版社

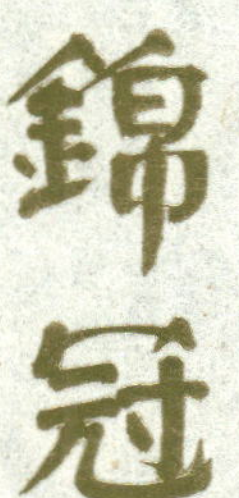

The Acme of All Brocades

Nanjing Yunjin Brocade and Silk-weaving Archives Picture Album

南京云锦及丝织业档案图典

南京市档案馆　编

　　南京丝织业历史悠久、繁荣兴盛，元代有东、西织染局，明代有内织染局，清代的江宁织造府是江南三大织造之一。近现代以来，以中兴源丝织厂为代表的丝织业工厂延续了旧时的辉煌。

　　南京云锦代表了传统手工丝织技艺的最高成就，她一端承载着中国深厚悠久的历史文化，另一端则影响着当代中国丝织业的发展，其传统织造技艺延续至今。2009年，南京云锦木机妆花织造技艺被联合国教科文组织列入《人类非物质文化遗产代表作名录》。

　　2019年，南京市档案馆在挖掘整理馆藏档案的基础上，联合中国第二历史档案馆、南京轻纺产业（集团）有限公司、江宁织造博物馆、南京江南丝绸文化博物馆、南京正源兴服饰设计有限公司等单位共同开展了南京云锦及丝织业档案的收集、整理与研究工作。同年，《南京云锦及丝织业档案》被列入国家档案局"十三五"国家重点档案保护与开发项目。本书是该项目重要成果之一。

　　本书汇集了南京市档案馆馆藏中兴源丝织厂的档案，江宁织造博物馆收藏的珍贵云锦实物，正源兴绸缎庄保存的部分云锦大师作品，以及江南丝绸文化博物馆的云锦数字化保护成果，既有不同历史时期的云锦和意匠藏品，又有反映其工艺技术流程、特征的代表作，分专题结合时间排列，简要介绍名称、工艺技术、时代特征和艺术内涵，以图文并茂的方式呈现给读者。

　　本书中所有云锦实物及图稿所标记的年代为其生产形成年代，相当一部分纹样源自元、明、清的传世经典纹样。

　　本书首次跨领域实现了云锦档案和文物的汇集；首次跨时代梳理了元、明、清时期到近现代完整的云锦发展历程；首次跨维度搭建了档案馆、博物馆、高校、云锦大师协同的档案保护工作平台。以保护文化遗产、传承文化基因为初心，打造了一个档案活化保护领域的"南京模式"。

　　回首南京云锦兴衰历程，鲜艳绚丽的颜色也许会在时间长河中褪去了光彩，经纬交错的图案纹样也许会在岁月蹉跎中模糊了肌理，但是南京云锦作为人类的非物质文化遗产，她的成就、智慧不应在时代的潮流中暗淡了光芒。只有让更多的人读懂南京云锦的独特魅力，她才能永远鲜活下去。探索、发现、传承、创新云锦的技艺和文化，是当代守护者的历史责任。

Nanjing silk-weaving industry, spanning a long history, has enjoyed great prosperity. There were East and West Weaving and Dyeing Bureaus in the Yuan Dynasty, and Internal Weaving and Dyeing Bureau in the Ming Dynasty, and Jiangning Imperial Silk-manufacturing Bureau was one of the three major weaving bureaus south of the Yangtze River. Since modern times, the silk-weaving factory, represented by Zhongxingyuan Silk-weaving Factory, has continued its past glory.

Nanjing Yunjin brocade represents the highest achievement of traditional manual silk-weaving skills. It bears the profound history and culture of China and influences the development of contemporary China's silk-weaving industry. It is a traditional weaving skill that has continued until now. In 2009, the weaving techniques of zhuanghua of Nanjing Yunjin brocade was listed in the Representative List of the Intangible Cultural Heritage of Humanity by UNESCO.

In 2019, on the basis of exploring the archives, Nanjing Archives carried out the collection, sorting and researching of Nanjing Yunjin brocade and silk-weaving archives, in cooperation with the Second Historical Archives of China, Nanjing Light Textile Industry Co., LTD., Jiangning Imperial Silk-manufacturing Museum, Nanjing Jiangnan Silk Culture Museum, Nanjing Cheng Yuan Hsing Fashion Design Co., LTD. In the same year, *The Archives of Nanjing Yunjin Brocade and Silk-weaving Industry* was listed in the "13th Five-year Plan" National Key Archives Protection and Development Projects by the National Archives Administration of China and this book was one of the important achievements.

This book collects the archives of Zhongxingyuan Silk-weaving Factory from Nanjing Archives, precious Yunjin brocades from Jiangning Imperial Silk-manufacturing Museum, some fine works of Nanjing Yunjin brocade masters preserved by Cheng Yuan Hsing, and the digital protection achievements of Yunjin brocade from Nanjing Jiangnan Silk Culture Museum. There are not only Yunjin brocades and mental composition collections in different periods, but also representative works reflecting their technical process and characteristics. The names, techniques, characteristics and artistic connotations are presented to the readers in the form of illustrations and texts, according to special topics and time periods. All the Yunjin brocades and drawings in this book are marked with the age of their formation, and a considerable part of the patterns come from the Yuan, Ming and Qing Dynasty.

This book realizes the first collection of Yunjin brocade archives and cultural relics. It is the first time to clarify the development process of Nanjing Yunjin brocade from the Yuan, Ming and Qing Dynasties to modern times. It is the first time to establish a platform of archive protection where archives, museums, universities and masters can cooperate. With the original intention of protecting cultural heritage and inheriting cultural genes, we have created a "Nanjing model" in the field of archives activation and protection.

Looking back on the history of Nanjing Yunjin brocade, although the bright colors and the patterns of warp yarn and weft yarn may fade in the long passage of time, the achievements and wisdom of the Yunjin brocade, as the intangible cultural heritage of mankind, should not be dimmed by the trend of the times. Only by guiding more people to understand the unique charm of Yunjin brocade, can it remain vigorous forever. So the historical responsibility of the contemporary guardian is to explore, discover, inherit and innovate the skills and the culture of Nanjing Yunjin brocade.

南京云锦品种和工艺在历史的发展长河中不断地丰富和提高，云锦织造技艺更是达到了传统手工丝织技艺的顶峰，逐步形成了自己独特的一套美学体系。

中国古代"天人合一"的思想，皇权与吉祥文化的定式，对美好生活的向往，这些都非常巧妙地融入云锦鲜活的纹样和千变万化的色彩中。云锦的设计以吉祥、奢华为主要特点，常以花卉、果实、走兽、游鳞以及佛教和仙道宝物为主要设计题材，历代创造无数经典纹样。云锦图案设计讲究图必有意、意必吉祥，人们常以"仙鹤"祝寿、以"葫芦"取其谐音寓意"福禄"、以"牡丹"象征富贵吉祥，体现出国人"至真淳朴，娴静不躁"的生活态度。云锦色彩艳丽且丰富，具有强烈的视觉效果，匠人通过优化线条、提炼图案元素、创作非现实题材等手法进行再设计，使云锦图案呈现出繁花似锦的艺术效果。

清代江宁织造府是专供皇家御用的丝织品生产机构，尤其以云锦著称。如今云锦的使用早已超越阶层、时间和空间的束缚，走入寻常百姓家。现代云锦的设计已经广泛应用于服饰、装饰品、工艺品等多种日常用途。不断的工艺创新提升了艺术表达能力，部分品种的图案所呈现的人物和场景还具有一定的立体感，可以生动地表现传统故事画面。本章精选了部分经典实物及意匠手稿，引领读者感受以云锦为代表的织物之美。

The Majestic Beauty of Nanjing Yunjin Brocade

In the long passage of time, Nanjing Yunjin brocade has become greatly diversified in variety and technique and the fabricating techniques of Nanjing Yunjin brocade go so far as to reach the summit of traditional manual silk-fabricating techniques, bringing forth a unique system of aesthetics.

The vibrant patterns and diverse colors of Nanjing Yunjin brocade have absorbed in an elaborate manner such elements as unity of man and nature, a prevailing notion since China's ancient times, imperial power and models of auspicious culture, and longing for an improved life. The design of Nanjing Yunjin brocade is characterized by auspice and luxury, featuring flowers, fruits, beasts, scales, and treasures in Buddhist and Taoist ideologies, and innumerable classical patterns have come into being accordingly over the centuries. The design of Nanjing Yunjin brocade lays special emphasis on the underlying auspicious implications: cranes are applied to congratulate an elderly on his birthday, bottle gourds to evoke associations with fortune and wealth, peonies to symbolize wealth and auspice. All the patterns are indicative of Chinese people's innocence, tranquility and peace. Nanjing Yunjin brocade, which is affluent in bright colors, is able to produce strong visual effects. The craftsmen are capable of bringing forth an artistic effect of various flowers unfolding, by means of perfecting the lines, highlighting the essential elements and creating non-realistic themes.

Jiangning Imperial Silk-Manufacturing Bureau is a production organ where silk fabrics intended only for imperial use are manufactured, and among others, Nanjing Yunjin brocade is the most reputable. Nowadays, Nanjing Yunjin brocade has already gone beyond the limits imposed by social strata, time and space, and has gradually found its place in ordinary households. The modern design of Nanjing Yunjin brocade has been widely applied to clothing, ornaments, art-wares and other everyday aspects. Improving innovation in techniques promotes artistic expressiveness. The patterns on part of the categories reveal figures and scenes which are third-dimensional, taking on scenes of vivid stories. This chapter selects and compiles a portion of classical brocade works and mental compositions, with the intention to guide the audience to appreciate the beauty of such fabrics as Nanjing Yunjin brocade.

该云锦用色绒和金线织成纹样，上下交错横向排列，两排为一个循环，为『整剖光』格式排列。

在一定区域内的莲花配色各不相同，术语称为『逐花异色』。

每朵莲花饱满无枝、左右对称，图案风格源于明代。大洋莲纹样的形成是东西方文化交流的结果，后成为云锦经典纹样之一。

Name   Two pieces of Dayang lotus pattern zhuanghua satin with red ground
Years   1950s
Collection   Nanjing Archives
Size   Length: 60 cm Width: 78 cm

名称　红地二则大洋莲纹妆花缎

年代　1950 年代

收藏　南京市档案馆

尺寸　长 60 厘米　宽 78 厘米

The brocade is made by colored velvet and gold thread, which are staggered horizontally from top to bottom. Two rows form a cycle, which is arranged in the format of zhengpouguang.

Different colors of lotus are in a certain area, which is called "different colors by flowers".

Each lotus is blooming without branches and symmetric. The pattern style is originated from the Ming Dynasty. The formation of Dayang lotus is the result of cultural exchanges between East and West, and has become one of the classic patterns of Nanjing Yunjin brocade.

该云锦用五彩色绒织成蔷薇花主体纹饰，图案设计创新性的运用了写实的表现形式，提升了花卉的美感。

花瓣采用对卡晕的手法表现色彩过渡，并以金线勾出花瓣和叶片的轮廓，花朵大小不一，有的完全盛开，有的含苞待放，整体图案的韵律节奏完美统一。

名称　蓝地二则串枝蔷薇花纹妆花缎
年代　1960 年
收藏　南京市档案馆
尺寸　长 410 厘米　宽 78 厘米

Name　Two pieces of twig rose pattern zhuanghua satin with blue ground
Years　1960
Collection　Nanjing Archives
Size　Length: 410 cm　Width: 78 cm

The brocade is using rose as the main decoration with colorful woven velvet. The pattern is creatively designed by the forms of realistic expression, which have enhanced the beauty of flowers.

The petals exhibit the color transition by the method of blocking halo, and hook the outline of petals and leaves with gold thread. The flowers are of different sizes, some in full bloom and some in budding, which could form a perfectly unified rhythm of the overall pattern.

该云锦用圆金线铺地，用五彩色绒织成牡丹纹，三朵牡丹及小花点缀形成一个团窠，扁金线铺团窠底，使之更加醒目突出，富有层次效果。团窠之间以一束牡丹妆点空白处，构图匀称。金宝地织物用金量大，为云锦珍贵品种之一。

名称　二则五彩牡丹纹金宝地
年代　1964 年
收藏　南京市档案馆
尺寸　长 1024 厘米　宽 61 厘米

Name　Two pieces of colorful peony pattern on golden ground
Years　1964
Collection　Nanjing Archives
Size　Length: 1024 cm Width: 61 cm

The brocade uses round gold thread as the bottom, and colorful velvet to form peony pattern. Three peonies and small flowers form a round cluster, and flat gold thread is used as the bottom of the cluster. It produces more striking and stereoscopic effect.

A bunch of peonies are decorated in the empty space between the clusters, which leads to the symmetrical composition. The brocade uses a large amount of gold and is one of the most precious varieties of Nanjing Yunjin brocade.

该云锦以上下两排狮子为一个纵向纹样单位，上排狮子俯身张嘴，翘尾嬉戏，下排狮子昂首相对，形成双狮戏绣球状，云纹镶嵌其间，同一排狮子以挖花技艺配出不同色彩。锦面五彩缤纷，丰富饱满，喜庆祥瑞。

名称　蓝地四则双狮戏球纹妆花缎
年代　1960 年代
收藏　南京市档案馆
尺寸　长 135 厘米　宽 77 厘米

Name　Four pieces of double lion playing ball pattern zhuanghua satin with blue ground
Years　1960s
Collection　Nanjing Archives
Size　Length: 135 cm Width: 77 cm

The two rows of lions are used as a pattern unit for the circulation in the brocade. The upper lions bend over, open the mouth and play with tails up in the air. The lower lions hold their heads up and face each other, with both lions playing with the embroidered ball. Cloud patterns are interwoven between the lions. Lions in the same row are adorned with different colors by means of a special technique. So the brocade really abounds in color and auspicious implications.

该锦面妆金妆彩，用扁金线织出亮丽的卷叶，卷叶巧妙变形构成一个个团窠，在团窠内用色绒金线妆织牡丹和葡萄纹，让色彩多变的牡丹产生了节律感，画面统一和谐，象征富贵长寿、子孙昌盛。

名称　蓝地二则卷叶牡丹纹妆花缎
年代　1960 年代
收藏　南京市档案馆
尺寸　长 106 厘米　宽 85 厘米

Name　Two pieces of rolling leaf peony pattern zhuanghua satin with blue ground
Years　1960s
Collection　Nanjing Archives
Size　Length: 106 cm Width: 85 cm

The brocade is decorated with gold and colorful thread. Rolling leaves are woven with flat gold threads, which ingeniously form a group of circles. Peonies and grape patterns are decorated by colored velvet and gold thread in the circles, giving the colorful peonies a sense of rhythm and making this brocade uniform and harmonious. It symbolizes wealth, longevity and fruitful posterity.

该云锦用色绒织莲花及如意卷叶，金线除包边外还织莲子及枝条。

莲花花瓣为二晕设计，配色少重复。莲花上下交错横向排列，两排为一纹样循环，上下呼应构成四方连续图案。

莲纹在与民间文化融合的过程中，被赋予了『莲多子』的寓意。

名称　蓝地四则缠枝莲纹妆花缎
年代　1960 年代
收藏　南京市档案馆
尺寸　长 270 厘米　宽 78 厘米

Name   Four pieces of intertwined lotus pattern zhuanghua satin with blue ground
Years   1960s
Collection   Nanjing Archives
Size   Length: 270 cm Width: 78 cm

The brocade is constituted with lotuses and Ruyi curly leaves made of colored velvet, and lotus seeds and branches are woven with gold threads, which also serve to circle the brims.

The lotus petals are in two halos, which could reduce repetition in colors. The lotuses are staggered horizontally and two rows form a pattern cycle. The upper part and lower part form a consistent and corresponding pattern on all four sides.

The lotus patterns gradually develop the implication of more children in Chinese folk culture.

这是一幅以妆花工艺织成的工笔画风格的云锦作品，画面中的牡丹花、丁香树、绶带鸟相映成趣，风格雅致。左下角织有两枚印章，其中方印为『南京艺新丝织厂』印。此幅作品可装裱为云锦工艺品。

名称　白地绶带鸟牡丹纹妆花缎
年代　1972 年
收藏　南京市档案馆
尺寸　长 100 厘米　宽 35 厘米

Name   Ribbon bird and peony pattern zhuanghua satin with white ground
Years   1972
Collection   Nanjing Archives
Size   Length: 100 cm Width: 35 cm

The brocade is a Yunjin brocade work in the style of meticulous brushwork woven by zhuanghua techniques, the peonies, clove trees and ribbon birds in the brocade form an elegant contrast.

There are two seals woven in the lower left quarter, and on the square seal are characters "Nanjing Yixin Silk-weaving Factory".

The work can be mounted as a Yunjin brocade handicraft.

该云锦主体纹饰为龙凤纹，汲取了明、清龙凤纹的经典表现手法，龙凤灵动，色彩艳丽，环以五彩如意云纹、火珠、花卉等图案，形成了龙飞凤舞的艺术效果。龙凤纹自古以来为中国传统吉祥图案，是古代皇权的象征，也是最具代表性的云锦经典纹样之一，取其『龙凤呈祥』之意，通常用在大婚、庆典等重要场合。

名称　绿地独幅龙凤祥云纹妆花缎

年代　1970 年代

收藏　南京市档案馆

尺寸　长 145 厘米　宽 78 厘米

Name　Single piece of dragon, phoenix and auspicious cloud pattern zhuanghua satin with green ground

Years　1970s

Collection　Nanjing Archives

Size　Length: 145 cm　Width: 78 cm

The main patterns of the brocade are dragon and phoenix, which draws on the classic expression techniques in Ming and Qing dynasties. The dragon and phoenix are flexible and colorful, surrounded by colorful Ruyi clouds, fire beads, flowers and other patterns, and forming an artistic effect of flying dragon and dancing phoenix.

Dragon and phoenix pattern has been a traditional auspicious pattern in China since ancient times, and is a symbol of imperial power, representative of classic patterns of Yunjin brocade. The patterns are usually used on such important occasions as wedding and celebration.

该云锦主体纹饰为升、降龙和莲花，龙纹由色绒和金线织成，形态灵活生动；莲花敦厚饱满且硕大，色彩艳丽。整幅作品大气磅礴，端庄威严，富丽堂皇。

名称　红地独幅龙莲纹妆花缎

年代　现代

收藏　南京市档案馆

尺寸　长 80 厘米　宽 78 厘米

Name　Single piece of dragon and lotus pattern zhuanghua satin with red ground

Years　Modern

Collection　Nanjing Archives

Size　Length: 80 cm　Width: 78 cm

The main patterns of the brocade are ascending and descending dragons and lotus flowers. The dragon pattern is made of colored velvet and gold thread, and the shape is flexible and vivid. The lotus is succulent, in full bloom and with bright colors.

The whole work is magnificent, dignified and imposing.

该云锦用色绒和金线织成龙、凤、仙鹤、麒麟四个瑞兽禽鸟团纹，间饰八宝纹。

团纹上下两排为一个循环，纵向交错排列，

此为云锦典型的『匀罗摆』格式排列，寓意吉祥如意，喜庆安康。

名称　红地独幅八宝四灵仙纹妆花缎
年代　现代
收藏　南京市档案馆
尺寸　长 80 厘米　宽 78 厘米

Name　Single piece of eight treasures and four spirits divinity pattern zhuanghua
　　　satin with red ground
Years　Modern
Collection　Nanjing Archives
Size　Length: 80 cm　Width: 78 cm

The brocade is woven with colored velvet and gold thread into four auspicious animal patterns of dragon, phoenix, crane and unicorn, interspersed with eight treasures.

The upper and lower rows of the Tuan pattern are in a cycle, staggered vertically.

This is a traditional Yunjin pattern called "yun luo bai", which implies good luck and happiness.

该云锦纹样以五彩色绒和金线织造而成。设计上采用上下交错横向排列，两排为一个循环。

主体图案为双鱼，「鱼」取其谐音「余」，寓意好事连绵不断，富贵有余之意；

桃子、佛手、石榴图案构成「三多」，象征多寿、多福、多子，均为中国传统吉祥图案。

名称　红地二则福寿三多吉庆双鱼纹妆花缎

年代　现代

收藏　南京市档案馆

尺寸　长 75 厘米　宽 76 厘米

Name　Two pieces of longevity, happiness, and auspicious double fish
　　　pattern zhuanghua satin with red ground

Years　Modern

Collection　Nanjing Archives

Size　Length: 75 cm　Width: 76 cm

The brocade pattern is made of colorful velvet and gold thread. The design applies staggered horizontal arrangement from top to bottom, and two rows form one cycle. The main pattern is two fishes, and "fish" is associated with "Yu" in Chinese, which means good luck keeps coming, and wealth and honor are sufficient. Peach, bergamot and pomegranate patterns constitute the "three multitudes", which symbolize longevity, happiness and fertility. They are all traditional auspicious patterns in China.

该锦面配色清雅，以色绒织人物，金银线勾勒云纹、人物服饰上的纹饰及远处的建筑屋顶，形成立体效果。图案人物为洛神，展现了其身姿婀娜、楚腰蛴领之态，栩栩如生。

名称　月白地洛神妆花缎
年代　1956 年
收藏　南京市档案馆
尺寸　长 77 厘米　宽 78 厘米

Name　Luoshen zhuanghua satin with lunar-white ground
Years　1956
Collection　Nanjing Archives
Size　Length: 77 cm　Width: 78 cm

The color of the brocade is elegant. The characters of the brocade are woven with colored velvet, while the clouds, the patterns on the costumes and the distant buildings are outlined with gold and silver thread, which form a three-dimensional effect.

The figure in the pattern is "luoshen", a traditional Chinese beauty, which vividly displays her graceful posture, elegant waist and impeccable beauty.

该云锦通过浓艳的配色和刚劲有力的线条，生动展现《水浒传》中武松打虎的经典场景。

此作品摆脱平面设计的传统，具有场景感，是极具时代特征的云锦妆织画。

名称　古月地武松打虎妆花缎
年代　1972 年
收藏　南京市档案馆
尺寸　长 155 厘米　宽 78 厘米

Name　Wu Song fighting with a tiger pattern zhuanghua satin with pale bluish-white ground
Years　1972
Collection　Nanjing Archives
Size　Length: 155 cm　Width: 78 cm

The brocade vividly shows the classic scene of Wu Song (a Chinese traditional hero) fighting with a tiger in *Story by the Water Margin* through its colorful and strong lines.

This work innovates the traditional graphic design and conveys a sense of reality. It is a characteristic Yunjin weaving painting, which is typical of its times.

该云锦画面线条动感流畅，人物神态逼真，彩云环绕，金线充分起到画龙点睛的作用，风格新颖典雅，生动表现了中国经典民间传说『牛郎织女鹊桥相会』的场景。右下角织有『中国南京云锦』印。

名称　古月地牛郎织女妆花缎

年代　1972 年

收藏　南京市档案馆

尺寸　长 178cm　宽 78cm

Name　The Cowherd and the Girl Weaver pattern zhuanghua satin with pale bluish-white ground

Years　1972

Collection　Nanjing Archives

Size　Length: 178 cm　Width: 78 cm

The lines of the brocade are dynamic and smooth, the characters are lifelike, and the clouds are surrounding the two characters. The gold thread fully serves as the finishing touch. The style is novel and elegant, which shows the scene of "the Cowherd and the Girl Weaver meet on the magpie bridge".

The lower right corner is woven with the seal of "Nanjing Yunjin brocade, China".

该云锦以粉色为地，织一朵盛开的牡丹，对称的凤居于两边。

帐沿配色清雅，构图规整，线条流畅，是中华人民共和国成立以后南京中兴源丝织厂生产的民用丝织产品之一。

名称　粉地凤戏牡丹纹云锦帐沿织成料
年代　1955 年
收藏　南京市档案馆
尺寸　长 101 厘米　宽 146 厘米

Name　Curtain edge of phoenix playing with peony pattern Yunjin brocade with pink ground
Years　1955
Collection　Nanjing Archives
Size　Length: 101 cm　Width: 146 cm

The brocade uses pink as the ground, and weaves a peony in full bloom with symmetrical phoenixes on both sides.

The brocade has elegant colors, regular composition and smooth lines. It is one of the silk products for civil use produced by Nanjing Zhongxingyuan Silk-weaving Factory since the establishment of the PRC.

该台布中间织黄白荷花组成的花环，四角荷花为紫、红两色，翠鸟点缀其间，四周辅以绿色连续荷花纹样做边，留白处以金线铺地，寓意「和和美美」。台布面料四周配有流苏，华丽美观、织地挺阔，极具装饰性效果。

名称　荷花纹金宝地台布
年代　1955 年
收藏　南京市档案馆
尺寸　长 102 厘米　宽 102 厘米

Name　Table cloth of lotus pattern on golden ground
Years　1955
Collection　Nanjing Archives
Size　Length: 102 cm　Width: 102 cm

A wreath composed of yellow and white lotuses is woven in the middle of the brocade. The lotuses in the four corners are purple and red, and kingfishers are interspersed among them. The brocade is surrounded by continuous green lotus patterns, and the remaining space is adorned with gold threads, which means harmony and beauty. There are tassels sewn around the brocade, more than gorgeous and far from floppy, which exhibit a decorative effect.

台毯主体花纹为凤凰和牡丹，形成团窠居于正中，四角配异色牡丹。

以五彩色绒织凤纹，金线勾勒凤纹和花纹边线，艳丽华贵。

凤鸟姿态灵动，居于构图上方，牡丹端居下方娇艳盛开。

整个画面中的牡丹配色各不相同，充分体现云锦色彩丰富之特点。

名称　米白地凤戏牡丹纹妆花缎台毯
年代　1959 年
收藏　南京市档案馆
尺寸　长 62 厘米　宽 70 厘米

Name　Table blanket of phoenix playing with peony pattern zhuanghua satin with beige ground
Years　1959
Collection　Nanjing Archives
Size　Length: 162 cm　Width: 70 cm

The main pattern of the brocade is phoenix and peony, forming a circle in the middle, with peonies in different colors in four corners.

The phoenix patterns are made of colorful velvet, and the body lines are outlined with gold thread, which is gorgeous and luxurious.

The phoenix has a smart posture, which is located in the middle. The peony, which is in full bloom, rests below the phoenix.

The colors of the peonies are different from one another in the whole picture, which reflects the rich color characteristics of Yunjin brocade.

该云锦由孔雀、月季、牡丹、蝴蝶等图案构成，呈对称排布，用云锦妆花工艺织造而成。被面上花卉色彩丰富，孔雀翎毛翠羽栩栩如生，蝴蝶环绕月季形成团花居于中间位置，呈现一派美好祥和之气。

名称　粉地孔雀花卉纹妆花缎被面织成料
年代　1960 年
收藏　南京市档案馆
尺寸　长 202 厘米　宽 144 厘米

Name   Quilt cover fabric of peacock and flower pattern zhuanghua satin with pink ground
Years   1960
Collection   Nanjing Archives
Size   Length: 202 cm Width: 144 cm

The brocade is composed of peacock, rose, peony, butterfly and other patterns. It is symmetrically arranged and woven by zhuanghua skill of Yunjin brocade.

The flowers on the quilt surface are rich in color, the peacock feathers are green and lifelike, and the butterflies encircle the roses to form a cluster of flowers in the middle.

That exhibits a beautiful and peaceful atmosphere.

该意匠稿中心为二龙戏珠团窠，四角为凤戏牡丹纹，均为对称图案，寓意『龙凤呈祥』。

根据意匠背面注释，此为外销靠垫品种意匠稿。

名称　龙凤纹云锦意匠稿

年代　1989 年

收藏　南京市档案馆

尺寸　长 153 厘米　宽 149 厘米

Name　The mental composition of dragon and phoenix pattern zhuanghua satin

Years　1989

Collection　Nanjing Archives

Size　Length: 153 cm　Width: 149 cm

The center of the brocade is a pattern of two dragons playing with a bead, and in the four corners are patterns of phoenix playing with peonies. All of them are symmetrical patterns, implying auspice.

According to the notes on the back, it is the mental composition of cushion to be exported.

　　南京云锦素有"寸锦寸金"之称，与四川蜀锦、苏州宋锦并称为中国三大名锦，是中国古代优秀织造技艺的代表，多用于皇家御用品和赏赐用品。

　　云锦根据工艺特点可分为四个大类：妆花、织金、库锦、库缎。"妆花"是南京云锦中织彩最多、最华美的品种，在织造过程中用到束综分色提花，小纬管局部挖花盘织工艺，简称"妆织"。"织金"指织物的所有图案花纹全部用金属线（金线、银线）织出，不含彩纬（纹纬），纬向只含有地纬和金线两种材料，属于纬二重织物。"库锦"是由重组织织制而成的高级多彩的传统提花丝织物。"库缎"一般为单经单纬、经面缎地、纬面起花织物，有的品种局部加织一组金银线或花纬而形成局部重纬组织。

　　云锦以蚕丝为主要原料，辅以金银线、孔雀羽线等稀有珍贵之物，工艺独特，对织造操作技术要求很高。织制云锦需由织花工和拽花工两人相互配合，用传统的花楼木机织造。拽花工坐在花楼织机上，根据花本顺序提拉纤线形成花纹开口，织花工坐在机下，负责妆金敷彩。传统云锦匹料通常在缎首处织有字牌，标记生产厂家的字号，形成早期的品牌意识。云锦生产工序繁杂，主要有纹样设计、意匠填绘、挑花结本、原料准备、装机和织造等几个流程。本章中专门有一节以南京市档案馆馆藏档案"中兴源八宝团龙妆花缎"复制项目为例为读者详细解读云锦生产工艺流程。

The Acme of All Brocades

The Nanjing Yunjin brocade, reputed for its expensiveness, is reckoned as one of the three most famous brocades across China, along with Sichuan Figured Satin and Suzhou Song Brocade. It is representative of outstanding manufacturing skills in ancient China, which is mostly applied in wares for imperial use and emperors' rewards to subjects.

Nanjing Yunjin brocade, according to characteristics of techniques, falls into four categories: Zhuanghua, Zhijin, Kujin and Kuduan. Zhuanghua, the most colorful and splendid one among all sorts of Nanjing Yunjin brocade, applies sophisticated and elaborate techniques known as "zhuangzhi" in manufacturing process. Zhijin indicates that all the patterns and designs are formed by virtue of weaving the gold and silver threads, excluding colored threads. Horizontally, there are only wefts and gold threads and thus it is a sort of dual-weft fabric. Kujin is a kind of traditional silk fabric in multiple colors with highly advanced fabricating skills of dual weaving. Kuduan is usually single weft yarn plus single warp yarn, and the warp side is used as the background while the weft side is used to weave patterns. Some of its varities have gold and silver threads weaved in parts of its pattern.

Nanjing Yunjin brocade is made mostly of silk, and gold and silver threads and feathers of peacocks are also complementary. Nanjing Yunjin brocade calls for unique techniques and has high demands for manufacturing techniques. To fabricate Nanjing Yunjin brocade, different workers have to cooperate on the traditional wooden weaving machine. One worker sits on top of the loom, dedicated to forming the bases of the patterns, and another worker sits down the machine, taking charge of ornating the brocade with gold threads and colored velvet. Generally speaking, brocades are tagged with the name of the workshop from which fabrics are produced, which is indicative of a sense of intellectual property. Manufacturing Nanjing Yunjin brocade consists of many complex procedures, to name a few, designing patterns, drawing mental compositions, cross stitch knotting, preparing raw materials, installing weaving machines and weaving. This chapter intends to elaborate on the process of brocade production, by means of exemplifying a replicate called "Zhongxingyuan eight treasures group dragon zhuanghua satin" in Nanjing Archives.

该云锦为清代宫廷纹样，多用于宫廷吉庆场合。

云龙满幅尺寸的设计给人以大气磅礴之感，加上五彩配色，庄严华贵。

名称　黄地独幅大云龙纹妆花缎
年代　1957 年
收藏　南京市档案馆
尺寸　长 110 厘米　宽 76 厘米

Name　One piece of big dragon and cloud zhuanghua satin with yellow ground
Years　1957
Collection　Nanjing Archives
Size　Length: 110 cm　Width: 76 cm

名称　黄地独幅大云龙纹妆花缎
年代　1957 年
收藏　南京市档案馆
尺寸　长 110 厘米　宽 76 厘米

The brocade adopts the pattern of the court of Qing Dynasty, which is usually applied in celebrations and banquets.

Full-size design of cloud and dragon adds to a sense of grandeur, coupled with multi-colors, making the brocade solemn and magnificent.

该面料用通经通纬的织造方法，因此同一排的花纹配色一致，整幅面料形成横向色同、纵向色变的配色效果，多用于帽沿、衣襟、服饰配料等。

名称　黄地小菱格纹彩库锦
年代　1950 年代
收藏　南京市档案馆
尺寸　长 180 厘米　宽 78 厘米

Name   Small diamond lattices pattern Caiku brocade with yellow ground
Years   1950s
Collection   Nanjing Archives
Size   Length: 180 cm Width: 78 cm

The brocade is woven in warp and weft, so the patterns and colors in the same row are consistent. The whole brocade exhibits the same horizontal color and different vertical colors. It is mostly used for hat brims, lapels, clothing materials and so on.

该锦面以五枚二飞经面缎地暗花纹织成，纹样为四合如意云龙纹，龙纹和云纹尺寸相近，并列交错排放，上下左右接章，中间饰有杂宝。多作服饰用料。

Name   Miscellaneous treasures, Ruyi, cloud and Dragon pattern Ku satin with red ground
Years   2015
Collection   Nanjing Jiangnan Silk Culture Museum
Size   Length: 110 cm Width: 78 cm

名称　红地杂宝四合如意云龙纹库缎
年代　2015 年
收藏　南京江南丝绸文化博物馆
尺寸　长 110 厘米　宽 78 厘米

The brocade is woven in a pattern with 5/2 satin. The pattern features cloud and dragon. The dragon pattern and the cloud pattern are similar in size and are arranged in a staggered manner. There are miscellaneous treasures in the middle of the brocade. This brocade is mostly used as clothing materials.

该锦面图案源于元代纳石失纹样，由水滴型单位团窠图案以『整剖光』格式排列而成。

团窠内上下为云和地，中间为卧姿鹿纹。面料华丽且贵重，装饰性极强。

名称　红地鹿纹滴珠窠织金锦
年代　2015 年
收藏　南京江南丝绸文化博物馆
尺寸　长 100 厘米　宽 78 厘米

Name　Brocade of deer pattern woven with gold threads in the shape of waterdrops with red ground
Years　2015
Collection　Nanjing Jiangnan Silk Culture Museum
Size　Length: 100 cm　Width: 78 cm

The pattern is derived from the Nasich pattern in the Yuan Dynasty. It features patterns of clusters of waterdrops, arranged in a manner of "zhengpouguang".

The upper and lower parts are clouds and the earth, and in the middle are crouching deers. The brocade is gorgeous, expensive and highly decorative.

八宝团龙妆花缎是根据南京市档案馆馆藏档案（手工意匠稿）复原而成。纹样单位尺寸长八十厘米，宽七十八厘米，主体纹饰为织金妆花团龙纹，周围环以五彩八宝，组成四方连续图案。

八宝又称『八瑞相』，由法轮、海螺、宝伞、宝盖、莲花、宝罐、双鱼、盘长八种吉庆祥瑞之物组成，寓意吉祥、幸福、圆满。

八宝团龙妆花缎复原周期长达十个月，严格按照云锦传统手工妆花工艺织造而成，充分体现了云锦『通经断纬、逐花异色』的特点。

意匠档案整理

对原始档案的清晰度进行调整，并裁剪出循环单位图案。

Arrangement of the mental composition archive
Adjust the clarity of the original file and cut out the circular unit pattern.

绘制线条稿

对意匠图原稿进行再整理，修正变形线条，绘制线条稿。

Drawing of line draft
Reorganize the mental composition, correct the deformed line, and draw a line draft.

绘制意匠稿

对照原件和线条稿绘制意匠稿，并根据图案色彩配出意匠用色，配色要考虑后期织造时方便织手对"逐花异色"的操作。

Draw the mental composition
Compare the original mental composition and line draft, and match the color according to the pattern colors. The color matching should take into account the convenience of the weaver to operate "different colors by flowers" during later weaving.

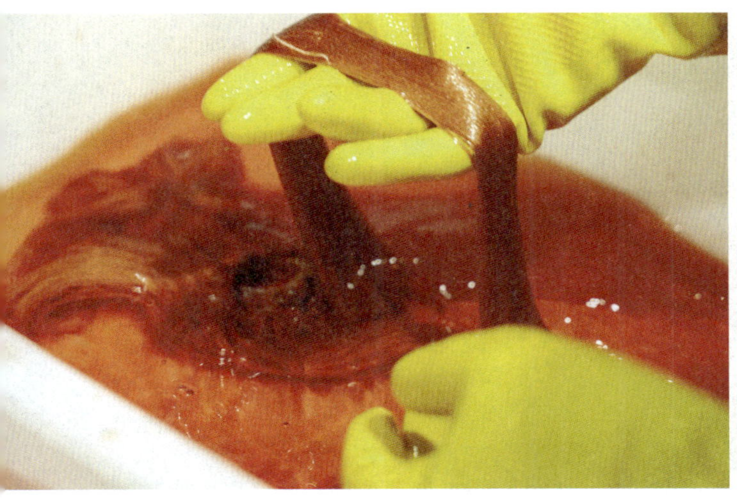

染色

将白色丝线浸入天然矿物染料或植物染料中，根据所需颜色的深浅，经过反复浸泡、过滤、固色等步骤完成染色。

Dyeing

Immerse traditional white silk yarns into dyes made of natural minerals and herbs, and carry out the whole process of repeatedly immersing, filtering, and stablizing the colors, according to the requirements of colors.

配色

根据配色选取色绒，为织造做准备工作。

Color matching

Select colored velvet according to color matching, and prepare for weaving.

挑花结本

在挑花架上用挑花钩手工挑制花本，将意匠稿上图案的位置和色彩的信息编制进经纬结构的花本当中。

Cross stitch knot

Handpicked flower books are made on the flower picking rack, and the information about the position and color of the patterns on the design manuscript is compiled into flower books made of special cotton thread.

织造

大花楼织机是云锦生产的专用织机，整个织造过程由拽花工提花，织花工投梭过管，两人共同配合完成。

Weaving

Dahualou loom is the special loom for Yunjin brocade production. The whole weaving process needs two people.

下机整理，完成织造。

Finishing

Eight treasures and group dragon zhuanghua satin Yunjin brocade is restored from the archives (handmade mental composition) in Nanjing Archives. The pattern is 80 cm long and 78 cm wide. The main part features group dragon pattern woven with gold threads, surrounded by colorful eight treasures, and forming a consistent pattern in four directions.

The eight treasures, also known as "eight auspicious symbols", are composed of eight auspicious objects, namely, wheel, conch shell, parasol, the marquee, lotus, the vase, double fish and endless knot, which imply luck, happiness and completeness.

The whole weaving restoration cycle of the Nanjing Yunjin brocade is up to 10 months, which strictly follows the traditional zhuanghua techniques of Nanjing Yunjin brocade. It reflects the distinctive characteristics of traditional Yunjin brocade zhuanghua craft, which is "connected warp, disconnected weft and different colors by flowers".

该云锦用捻金线织正卍字纹，湖色缎地。

缎首织有『江南织造臣庆林』及『机匠王援』的字样。

庆林，清同治年间任江南（宁）织造。

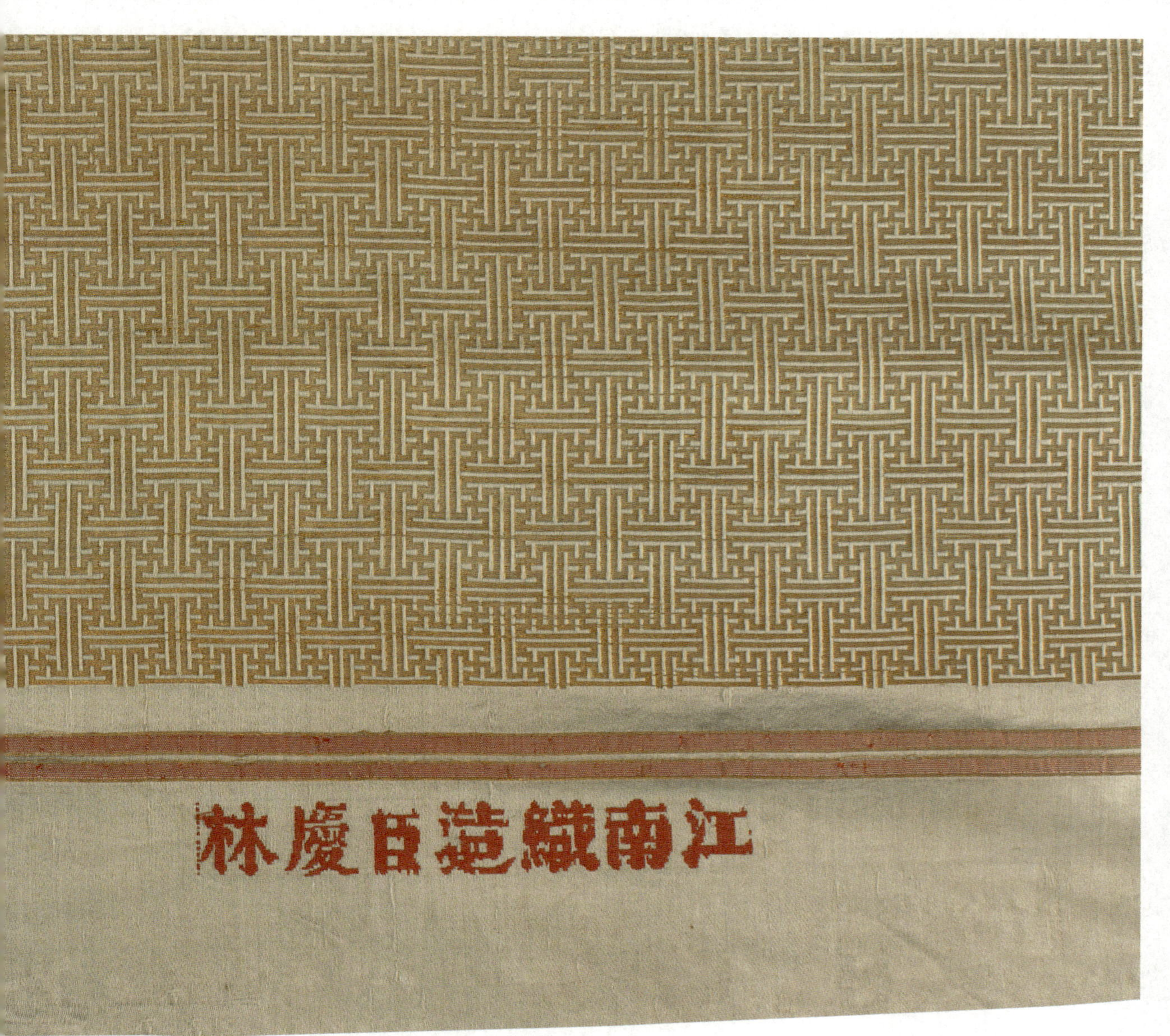

Name　卍 pattern brocade woven with gold threads with lake color ground
Years　Qing Dynasty
Collection　Jiangning Imperial Silk-manufacturing Museum
Size　Length: 1383 cm Width: 79 cm

名称　湖色地正卍字纹织金缎

年代　清

收藏　江宁织造博物馆

尺寸　长 1383 厘米　宽 79 厘米

The pattern is woven with twisted gold thread into 卍, with lake color as the satin's ground.

In the head of the satin are woven " 江南织造臣庆林 (Jiangnan weaving minister Qing Lin)" and " 机匠王援 (machine worker Wang Yuan)".

Qing Lin is a government official in charge of imperial silk-manufacturing south of the Yangtze River during the reign of Tongzhi Emperor of the Qing Dynasty.

该云锦用真圆金线织冰梅纹，青色缎地。

冰梅纹是将冰裂纹的肌理与梅花的线条图案完美结合，象征高洁雅致，颇具文人气息。

缎首织『方永泰本机真库金』字样。

Name   Ice plum pattern brocade woven with gold threads with green ground
Years   Qing Dynasty
Collection   Jiangning Imperial Silk-manufacturing Museum
Size   Length: 416 cm Width: 74.5 cm

名称　青地冰梅织金缎
年代　清
收藏　江宁织造博物馆
尺寸　长 416 厘米　宽 74.5 厘米

The brocade is made of round gold thread with ice plum pattern and blue satin.

Ice plum pattern is a combination of ice crack texture and plum blossom pattern, which symbolizes high purity and elegance. It creates an atmosphere of literati.

In the head of the satin, are woven " 方永泰本机真库金 (Fang Yongtai ben ji zhen ku jin)".

该云锦用织金技法织串菊纹，青色缎地，花朵饱满且有层次感，满地显金，青地色勾画菊纹轮廓线。

缎首织「金陵涂东元玉记库金」字样。

Name   String chrysanthemum pattern brocade woven with gold threads with green ground
Years   Qing Dynasty
Collection   Jiangning Imperial Silk-manufacturing Museum
Size   Length: 429 cm Width: 77 cm

名称　青地串菊织金缎

年代　清

收藏　江宁织造博物馆

尺寸　长 429 厘米　宽 77 厘米

The brocade is woven with gold-weaving techniques to string chrysanthemum patterns with blue satin. The flowers are in full bloom and have a layered feeling. The ground is covered with gold, and the blue color outlines the chrysanthemum patterns.

In the head of the satin, are woven "金陵涂东元玉记库金 (Jinling tudong yuanyuji ku jin)".

该云锦用织金技法织小团龙和杂宝纹，石青色缎地。

缎首织『两淮盐运使司盐运使』字样。

使運鹽都司使運鹽淮兩

名称　石青小团龙织金缎
年代　清
收藏　江宁织造博物馆
尺寸　长 1400 厘米　宽 76.5 厘米

Name　Small groups of dragons pattern brocade woven with gold threads with stone green color
Years　Qing Dynasty
Collection　Jiangning Imperial Silk-manufacturing Museum
Size　Length: 1400 cm　Width: 76.5 cm

名称　石青小团龙织金缎
年代　清
收藏　江宁织造博物馆
尺寸　长 1400 厘米　宽 76.5 厘米

The brocade uses gold-weaving techniques to weave small groups of dragons and miscellaneous treasure pattern with stone blue satin.

In the head of the satin, are woven " 两淮盐运使司盐运使 (Lianghuai yanyunshisi yanyunshi)".

该云锦用丝绒色线织五彩莲花，大量片金显叶纹，绿色缎地，缎首织『江南织造臣七十四』字样。

七十四，清道光三年（一八二三）年任江南（宁）织造。

Name   Multicolored lotus pattern flat gold satin with dark green ground
Years   Qing Dynasty
Collection   Jiangning Imperial Silk-manufacturing Museum
Size   Length: 686 cm Width: 73 cm

名称　深绿地五彩勾莲纹片金缎

年代　清

收藏　江宁织造博物馆

尺寸　长 686 厘米　宽 73 厘米

The brocade uses velvet thread to weave colorful lotus flowers, and uses a large number of golden patterns with leaves on them. In the head of the satin, are woven " 江南织造臣七十四 (Jiangnan Silk-manufacturing minister Qi Shisi)".

Qi Shisi is a government official in charge of the Jiangning Silk-manufacturing Bureau in the 3rd year (1823) of the reign of Daoguang Emperor in the Qing Dynasty.

该云锦用片金和色绒织五彩花卉，大红缎地，缎首织『杭州织造臣诚全』字样。

诚全，清光绪年间任杭州织造。

名称　大红五彩花卉纹片金缎
年代　清
收藏　江宁织造博物馆
尺寸　长 1343 厘米　宽 73.5 厘米

Name　Multicolored flower pattern flat gold satin with bright red ground
Years　Qing Dynasty
Collection　Jiangning Imperial Silk-manufacturing Museum
Size　Length: 1343 cm Width: 73.5 cm

The brocade is woven of flat thread gold and colored velvet into colorful flowers, with dark red satin as the ground. In the head of the satin, are woven " 杭州织造臣诚全 (Hangzhou weaving minister Cheng Quan)".

Cheng Quan is a government official in charge of Hangzhou silk-manufacturing during the reign of Guangxu Emperor of the Qing Dynasty.

该条幅底料为墨绿色凤穿牡丹纹雕花天鹅绒，匹头织有『江苏省南京市艺新丝织生产社』字牌。

雕花天鹅绒底料上贴有『南京云锦艺新丝织厂』字样的布贴，

布贴材质为锁甲纹织金锦。

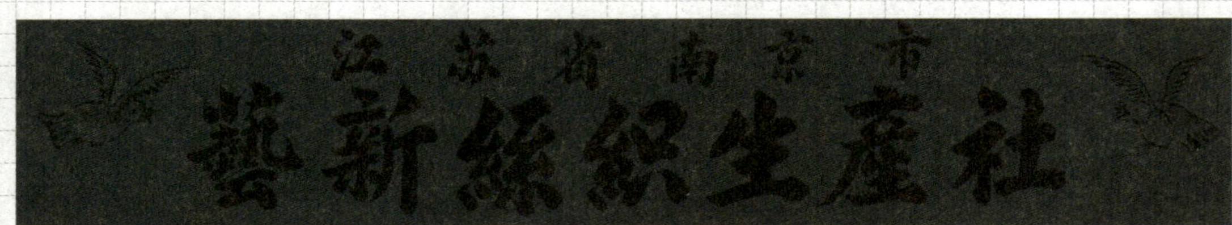

Name   Velvet sticker banners with blackish green ground
Years   1956
Collection   Nanjing Archives
Size   Length: 72 cm Width: 107 cm

名称　墨绿地天鹅绒贴字条幅
年代　1956 年
收藏　南京市档案馆
尺寸　长 72 厘米　宽 107 厘米

The backing material of this banner is floral velvet embroidered with dark green phoenix and peony pattern, on top of which are Chinese characters "江苏省南京市艺新丝织生产社 (Jiangsu Province Nanjing Yixin Silk-weaving Factory)".

On the backing material made of velvet ornate with flowers, is attached a sticker made of cloth, bearing "南京云锦艺新丝织厂 (Nanjing Yunjin brocade Yixin Silk-weaving Factory)". The sticker is made of brocade woven with gold threads with lock armour pattern.

据南京中兴源丝织厂厂史记载，一八七四年『正源兴绸缎庄』在北京创立，同年秋在南京地区开办其分号，选址南京绒庄街六十三号。

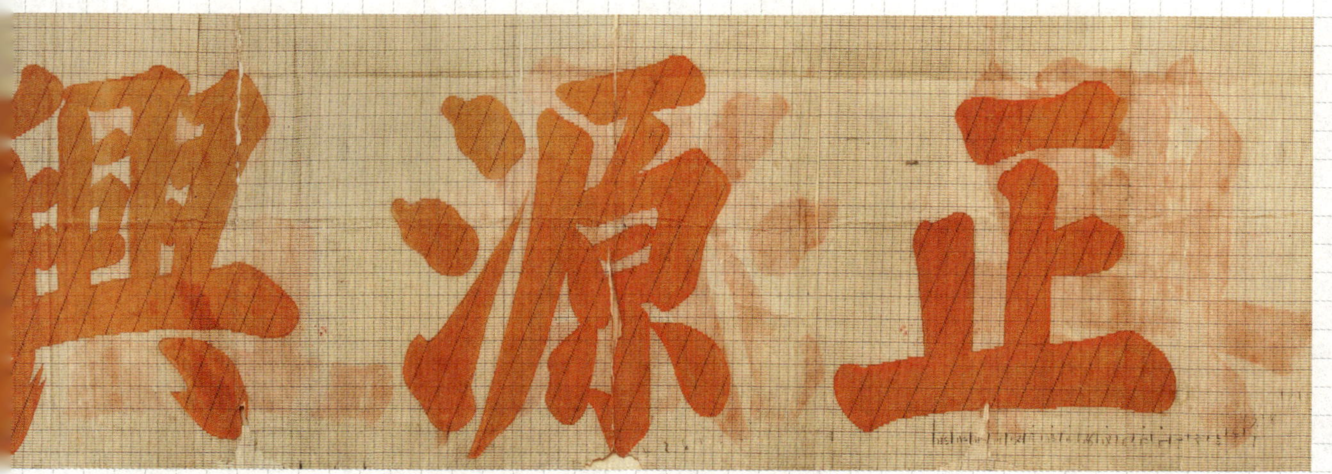

Name   The mental composition of " 正源兴厂督造 (supervised by Cheng Yuan Hsing Co., Ltd)" signboard
Years   1935
Collection   Nanjing Archives
Size   Length: 33 cm Width: 107 cm

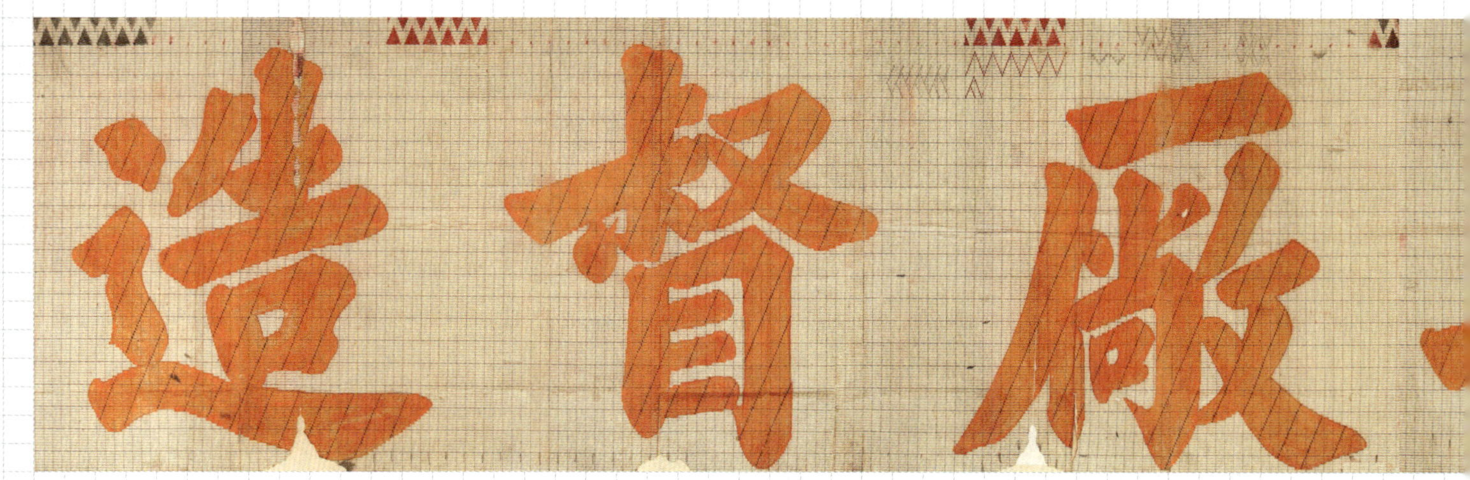

名称　"正源兴厂督造"字牌意匠稿
年代　1935 年
收藏　南京市档案馆
尺寸　长 33 厘米　宽 107 厘米

According to the history of Zhongxingyuan Silk-manufacturing Factory, Cheng Yuan Hsing Silk and Satin Shop was founded in Beijing in 1874. Its branch was founded in Nanjing in the same year, which was located in No.63 Rongzhuang street, Nanjing.

据南京中兴源丝织厂厂史记载，一九一三年，正源兴老掌柜李关之与南京人氏李柳堂、陈芦荪合股开办『中兴元缎号』，正式挂牌成立缎号。

一九二四年股东分股，李柳堂仍经营『中兴元缎号』，正源兴记将缎号『元』改为『源』，称为『中兴源缎号』经营。

一九四八年十月，北京正源兴号股东李氏兄弟分家，李思厚、李少镜、李致中、李思明等七人合股接下中兴源缎号的牌子，改缎号为丝织厂，易名为『中兴源丝织厂』。

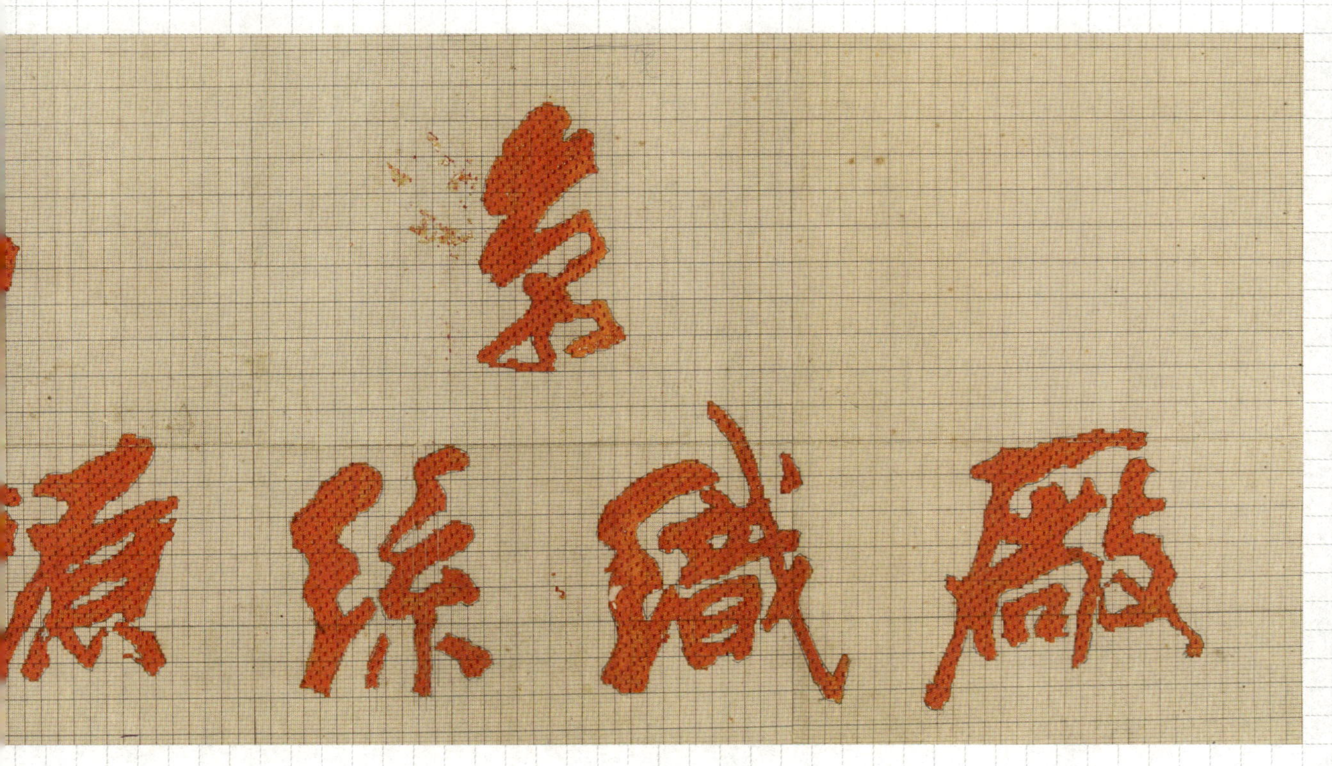

Name   The mental composition of "南京中兴源丝织厂 (Nanjing Zhongxingyuan Silk-weaving Factory)" signboard
Years   1982
Collection   Nanjing Archives
Size   Length: 37 cm Width: 85 cm

名称　"南京中兴源丝织厂"字牌意匠稿
年代　1982 年
收藏　南京市档案馆
尺寸　长 37 厘米　宽 85 厘米

According to the history of Zhongxingyuan Silk-weaving Factory, in 1913 Li Guanzhi, the manager of Cheng Yuan Hsing Co., Ltd. officially instituted a satin shop called Zhongxingyuan Satin Shop, in cooperation with two Nanjing local residents Li Liutang and Chen Lusun.

In 1924, the stockholders divided the share. While Li Liutang still ran the Zhongxingyuan Satin Shop, Cheng Yuan Hsing changed the Zhongxingyuan Satin (中兴元缎号) to Zhognxinyuan Satin (中兴源缎号).

In October 1948, Cheng Yuan Hsing Satin was divided among the Li brothers. Seven of the brothers, including Li Sihou, Li Shaojing, Li Zhizhong and Li Siming, jointly took over Zhongxingyuan Satin Shop, restructured it as a silk-weaving factory and the name was Zhongxingyuan Silk-weaving Factory.

元、明、清三代，云锦发展登峰造极。江南地区历来是全国丝织业的中心，南京(江宁)、苏州、杭州皆设有官办织造机构，被称为"江南三织造"。从发展规模和水平上看，南京的手工丝织业一直占据着城市产业的重要地位。

自民国开始，由于艺术家进入丝织品的设计领域，使得云锦的艺术设计和意匠稿题材更为多样，形式更为丰富。本章收录了大量云锦手工意匠及设计作品，题材多样、线条流畅、图案精巧、设计成熟，辅以翔实的技术说明，无不体现匠心所在。

中华人民共和国成立后，完整的云锦产业链逐渐形成。江南三地，在大型丝织厂的带动下，恢复了协同互补的产业模式。各厂家积极开发新品种，在设计上既能紧跟时代潮流，呼应宏大主题，又与生活日常结合，亲民实用。同时，由于大量丝织品的出口，云锦丝织业的图案纹样，也留下了对外交流、文化融合的印记。

二十世纪七八十年代，以中兴源为代表的丝织厂积极尝试将现代织机引入丝织品生产之中，在品种和原料上不断推陈出新，大大丰富了南京的丝织品种，迎来了南京丝织业的火红年代。

A History Spanning Centuries

The Yuan, Ming and Qing Dynasties witnessed the heyday of Nanjing Yunjin brocade. Historically, regions south of the Yangtze River have been the center for national silk industry. Nanjing, Suzhou and Hangzhou once set up official silk-manufacturing bureaus, which were renowned as "Three Manufacturing Bureaus South of the Yangtze River." In terms of scale and level, the manual silk industry in Nanjing has been incessantly playing a significant role in the city's industry.

During the ROC period, the artistic design and themes of mental compositions became diversified, owing to the influx of artists into the domain of artistic design. This chapter incorporates a considerable number of manual mental compositions and designs of the Nanjing Yunjin brocade, featuring various themes, smooth lines, elaborate patterns and sophisticated designs. Detailed technical instructions are complementary to this chapter as well. All is a reflection of the ingenuity and inventiveness of the craftsmen.

Since the founding of the People's Republic of China (PRC), an integrated industry chain of the Nanjing Yunjin brocade gradually came to existence. In Nanjing, Suzhou and Hangzhou, large silk-manufacturing factories gave impetus to an industry model in which factories are in coordination and collaboration with one another. Silk-manufacturing factories introduce innovations and are actively engaged in developing new categories. The design of Nanjing Yunjin brocade, as it turns out, keeps up with the trend of the times, and corresponds to grand themes, while it is also closely associated with everyday use and caters to household needs. In the meantime, thanks to the massive exportation of silk products, foreign exchange and cultural integration have also greatly affected the patterns of the Nanjing Yunjin brocade.

In the 1970s-80s, silk-manufacturing factories, sought to introduce modern weaving machines to the production of silk fabrics, and made strenuous efforts to innovate categories and materials. By so doing, the categories of the Nanjing Yunjin brocade are greatly enriched and a flowering epoch for the development of Nanjing silk industry is what we embrace.

纳石失是波斯语『织金锦』的音译词，是元代最具特色的特结型加金织物，使用两组经线，一组与地纬交织成地组织，另一组专门固结纹纬。蒙元贵族对这种中亚传统织物特别钟情，用其制作衣帽、帷幔、茵褥等，也常裁剪作为袄袍的领、袖缘，以显耀富足。

名称　纳石失金锦残片
年代　元
收藏　江宁织造博物馆

Name　Fragment of "Nasich" brocade
Years　Yuan Dynasty
Collection　Jiangning Imperial Silk-manufacturing Museum

"Nashishi" is a transliteration of Persian brocade woven with gold threads. It is the most distinctive gold adding fabric of the Yuan Dynasty. It uses two groups of warp threads, one group is interwoven with the ground weft yarn to form the ground organization, and the other group specifically consolidates the weft yarn.

The nobles of the Mongol and Yuan Dynasties were particularly fond of this kind of Central Asian traditional fabric. They used it to make clothes, hats, curtains, and umbrellas. They also often cut it out as the collar and sleeve edge of their jackets and robes to show their wealth.

该织片为明代皇家刻印大藏经的书衣封面，整体为长方形，周围裱装均为后人所补。可见原经册应为传统经折式装帧，这种装帧形式是隋唐佛教盛行时期，佛教徒为了唪诵经文的方便，而将佛经由以往的卷轴装改造形成的。

这件织锦片织造工艺细腻，金线纤细匀称，纹样典雅流畅，表现了明代高超的织锦技艺。

名称　明黄地龙凤纹妆花缎织片
年代　明
收藏　江宁织造博物馆
尺寸　长 29 厘米　宽 17 厘米

Name　The tapestry piece of dragon and phoenix pattern zhuanghua satin with bright yellow ground
Years　Ming Dynasty
Collection　Jiangning Imperial Silk-manufacturing Museum
Size　Length: 29 cm　Width: 17 cm

The tapestry piece is the cover of the Ming Dynasty's Royal engraving of the Tripitaka. The tapestry piece is rectangular, and the surrounding mounting is supplemented by later generations.

It can be seen that the original scriptures should be bound in a traditional folded manner. This kind of binding form was formed by Buddhists in the Sui and Tang Dynasties when Buddhism was prevalent. In order to facilitate the recitation of scriptures, the Buddhist scriptures were transformed from the previous scroll binding.

The weaving process of this brocade piece is exquisite, the gold thread is fine and symmetrical, and the pattern is elegant and smooth, which shows the superb brocade skills of the Ming Dynasty.

该云锦专为慈禧寿礼而作。在蓝色地上以五彩色绒织仙鹤纹样，上排仙鹤口衔寿桃，下排口衔灵芝，上下鹤首两两相对，周围饰有云纹，两排为一个循环。仙鹤、寿桃、云纹、灵芝配色各不相同，体现云锦妆花料『逐花异色』的显著特点。

名称　蓝地灵仙祝寿纹妆花缎
年代　清
收藏　南京市档案馆
尺寸　长 80 厘米　宽 77 厘米

Name　Treasures and immortals celebration zhuanghua satin with blue ground
Years　Qing Dynasty
Collection　Nanjing Archives
Size　Length: 80 cm　Width: 77 cm

The fabric is intended as the birthday gift of Cixi in the Qing Dynasty. The pattern is composed of colorful velvet with blue ground. The upper row of cranes hold longevity peaches in their mouths, and the lower row hold ganoderma in their mouths. The heads of the upper and lower cranes face each other in pairs, surrounded by cloud patterns. The two rows form a cycle.

Crane, longevity peach, cloud pattern and ganoderma have different colors, which reflects the remarkable feature of "different colors by flowers" of Yunjin brocade zhuanghua fabric.

该云锦用妆花技法满织缠枝牡丹莲纹，花型硕大饱满，缠枝婉转流畅，配色丰富、质地厚实。

名称　蓝地四则缠枝牡丹莲纹妆花缎
年代　近代
收藏　江宁织造博物馆
尺寸　长 180 厘米　宽 75 厘米

Name　Four pieces of intertwined lotus and peony pattern zhuanghua satin with blue ground
Years　Modern times
Collection　Jiangning Imperial Silk-manufacturing Museum
Size　Length: 180 cm　Width: 75 cm

The brocade is adorned with tangled lotus and peony patterns by zhuanghua techniques. The flowers are large and in full bloom, and the tangled branches are gentle and smooth. The color is rich, and the texture is thick.

该意匠稿原为南京中兴源丝织厂（南京中兴源绸厂）所有，背面记录有『苏州市纹工社绘』字样。

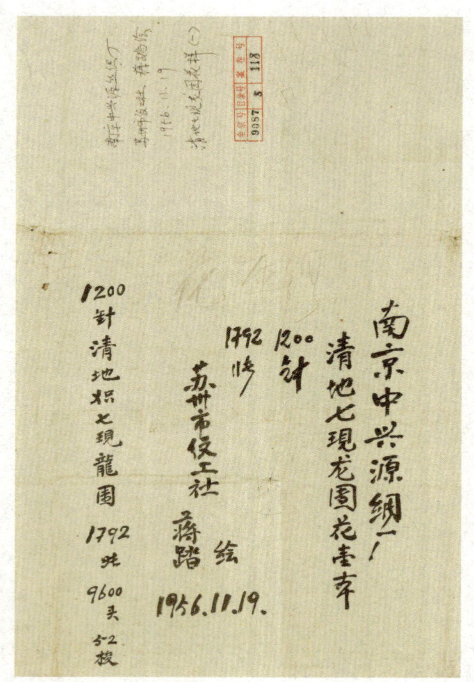

名称　清地七现龙团花纹意匠稿

年代　1956 年

收藏　南京市档案馆

尺寸　长 119 厘米　宽 100 厘米

Name　The mental composition of dragon pattern with natural colors

Years　1959

Collection　Nanjing Archives

Size　Length: 125 cm　Width: 60 cm

The mental composition belongs to Nanjing Zhongxingyuan Silk-weaving Factory, with the characters "苏州市纹工社绘 (painted by Suzhou Wengong Factory)" on the back.

该意匠稿原为南京中兴源丝织厂所有，背面记录有「南京云锦研究所供样」。

名称　凤穿牡丹纹雨花锦意匠稿
年代　1959 年
收藏　南京市档案馆
尺寸　直径 41 厘米

Name　The mental composition of phoenix and peony pattern yuhua brocade
Years　1959
Collection　Nanjing Archives
Size　Diameter: 41 cm

The mental composition belongs to Nanjing Zhongxingyuan Silk-weaving Factory, with the characters " 南京云锦研究所供样 (from Nanjing Yunjin Brocade Research Institute)" on the back.

该意匠稿原为南京中兴源丝织厂所有，背面记录有「杭州来样」。

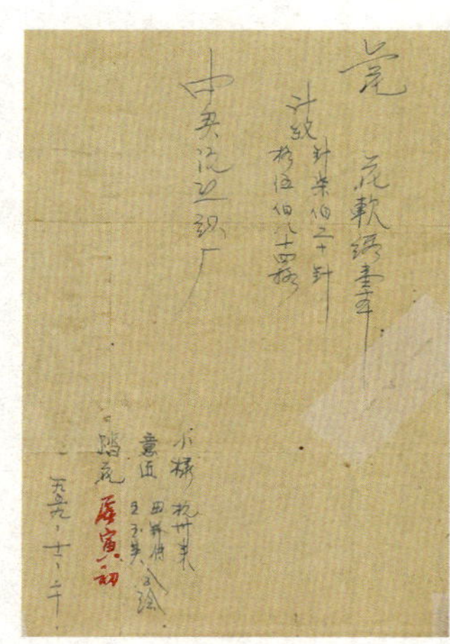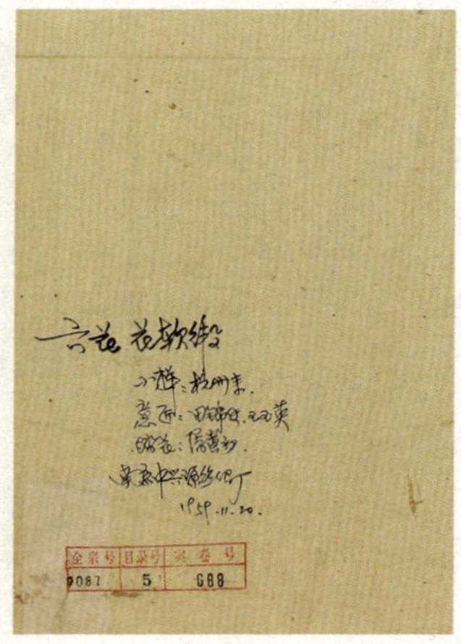

名称　花卉纹花软缎意匠稿
年代　1959 年
收藏　南京市档案馆
尺寸　长 125 厘米　宽 60 厘米

Name　The mental composition of floral pattern huaruan brocade
Years　1959
Collection　Nanjing Archives
Size　Length: 125 cm　Width: 60 cm

The mental composition belongs to Nanjing Zhongxingyuan Silk-weaving Factory, with the characters " 杭州来样 (from Hangzhou)" on the back.

该意匠稿设三色，线条流畅，构图自然，艺术高雅。原为南京中兴源丝织厂藏稿，背面记录有『锦华宝庄定＼（杭州）安祥纹社制』。

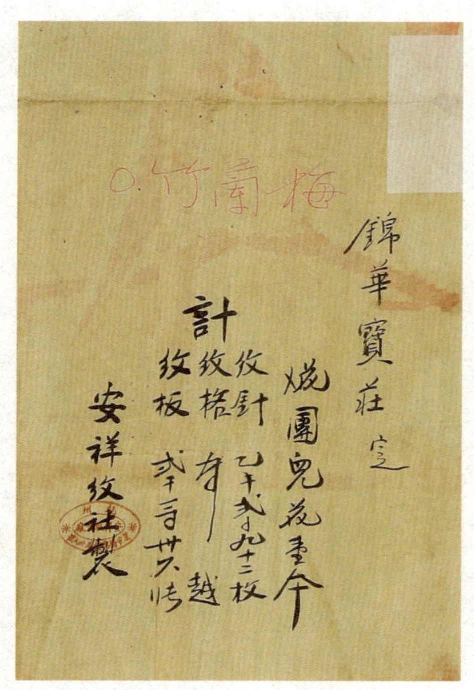

名称　团儿花竹兰梅纹意匠稿
年代　不详
收藏　南京市档案馆
尺寸　长 101 厘米　宽 93 厘米

Name　The mental composition of clustering bamboo, orchid and plum patterns
Years　Unknown
Collection　Nanjing Archives
Size　Length: 101 cm　Width: 93 cm

The mental composition has three colors, with smooth lines, natural composition, which makes it elegant. It is originally from NanjingZhongxingyuan Silk-weaving Factory, with the characters " 锦华宝庄定 /(杭州) 安祥纹社制 (required by Jin Hua Bao Zhuang/made by Anxiangwen Factory)" on the back.

该意匠稿设三色，传统文人题材，原为南京中兴源丝织厂藏稿，背面记录有『谢烈记宝厂＼美旦织物图案馆制』。

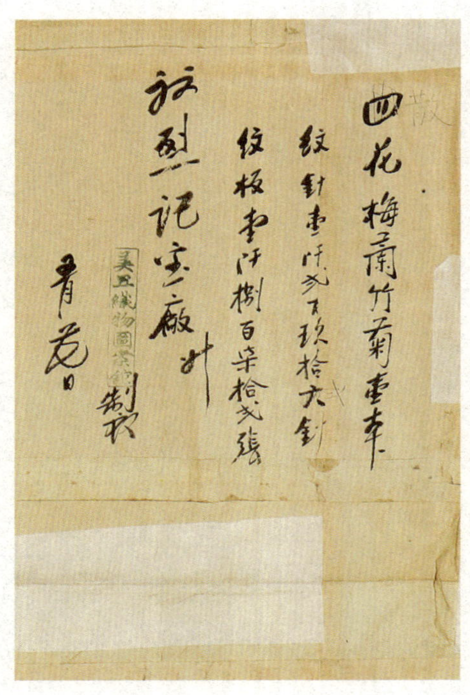

名称　梅兰竹菊纹意匠稿

年代　不详

收藏　南京市档案馆

尺寸　长 192 厘米　宽 110 厘米

Name　The mental composition of plum, orchid, bamboo and chrysanthemum patterns

Years　Unknown

Collection　Nanjing Archives

Size　Length: 192 cm　Width: 110 cm

The mental composition has three colors, and exhibits traditional literati themes. It is originally from NanjingZhongxingyuan Silk-weaving Factory, with the characters "谢烈记宝厂 / 美旦织物图案馆制 (made by Xieliejibao factory/Meidan Fabric Pattern Museum)" on the back.

该面料用妆花工艺临摹了二十世纪七十年代著名的宣传画『铁索桥畔』，人物线条刻画生动，配色自然纯朴，富有时代感。

名称　米白地铁索桥畔妆花缎
年代　1970 年
收藏　南京市档案馆
尺寸　长 77 厘米　宽 111 厘米

Name　Beside the iron-chain bridge zhuanghua satin with beige ground
Years　1970
Collection　Nanjing Archives
Size　Length: 77 cm　Width: 111 cm

铁索桥畔
天马奔途

The brocade imitates the famous picture "Beside the iron-chain bridge" in 1970s with zhuanghua skills. The characters are vividly depicted in lines, adopt strong colors, and is a reflection of the times.

此挂屏面料用妆花工艺织毛泽东诗词《沁园春·雪》，此料纬密较大，对书法的还原度较高，具有一定的收藏价值。

名称　米白地毛泽东诗词妆花缎挂屏
年代　1964 年
收藏　南京市档案馆
尺寸　长 58 厘米　宽 38 厘米

Name　Hanging screen of Mao Zedong's poems zhuanghua satin with beige ground
Years　1964
Collection　Nanjing Archives
Size　Length: 58 cm　Width: 38 cm

北国风光，千里冰封，万里雪飘。望长城内外，惟余莽莽；大河上下，顿失滔滔。山舞银蛇，原驰蜡象，欲与天公试比高。须晴日，看红装素裹，分外妖娆。

江山如此多娇，引无数英雄竞折腰。惜秦皇汉武，略输文采；唐宗宋祖，稍逊风骚。一代天骄，成吉思汗，只识弯弓射大雕。俱往矣，数风流人物，还看今朝。（沁园春）

The poem of Mao Zedong named "Qinyuan Spring · Snow" is woven with zhuanghua skills. The work applies multitudinous wefts, and is a vivid embodiment of the calligraphic work, which endow the work with great value for colletion.

此面料用单色纬织金陵饭店标志和字样，斜向四十五度排列，风格新颖独特。

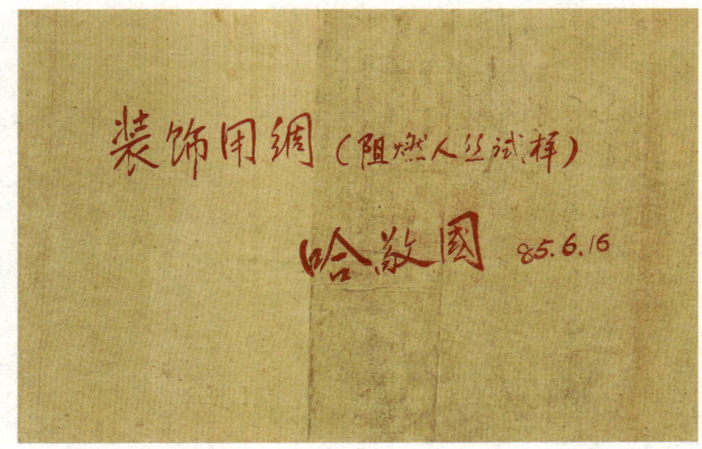

名称　金陵饭店字牌定制面料
年代　1985 年
收藏　南京市档案馆
尺寸　长 71 厘米　宽 80 厘米

Name　Jinling Hotel brand customized brocade
Years　1985
Collection　Nanjing Archives
Size　Length: 71 cm　Width: 80 cm

The brocade is woven with the logo and " 金 陵 饭 店 (Jinling Hotel)" customized for Jinlin Hotel, by means of weaving single-colored weft and gold brocade. The characters are arranged obliquely at 45 degree, which takes on a novel look.

该意匠稿以一九六八年南京长江大桥顺利通车为主题，是中兴源丝织厂（当时称作南京东方红丝织厂）响应时代热点的创新之作，充分体现南京特色。

名称　南京长江大桥软缎被面意匠稿
年代　1972 年
收藏　南京市档案馆
尺寸　长 82 厘米　宽 68 厘米

Name　The mental composition of soft satin quilt cover of Nanjing Yangtze River Bridge
Years　1972
Collection　Nanjing Archives
Size　Length: 82 cm　Width: 68 cm

The theme of the mental composition is the successful opening of Nanjing Yangtze River Bridge in 1968. It is an innovative work of Zhongxingyuan Silk-weaving Factory(called Dongfanghong Factory then) in response to the hotly-discussed topics of the times and fully reflects the characteristics of Nanjing.

南京中兴源丝织厂在二十世纪六十年代根据日本来样为日本客户定制衣料的手绘意匠稿。

构图简洁大方，为传统和风图案。

名称　竹叶纹妆花衣料意匠稿
年代　1967 年
收藏　南京市档案馆
尺寸　长 230 厘米　宽 112 厘米

Name　The mental composition of bamboo leaf pattern zhuanghua cloth brocade
Years　1967
Collection　Nanjing Archives
Size　Length: 230 cm　Width: 112 cm

The mental composition is customized by Nanjing Zhongxingyuan Silk-weaving Factory in the 1960s for Japanese clients.

The brocade is simple and generous, with traditional Japanese style pattern.

南京中兴源丝织厂根据捷克客户来样定制台布的意匠稿，图案设计为写实风格，通过绘制技法上的处理，可生动表现葡萄和叶片上的光影效果。

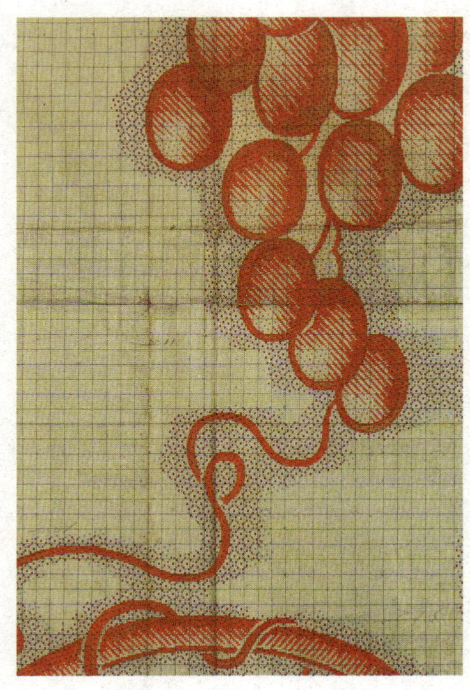

名称　葡萄纹面料意匠稿
年代　1960 年代
收藏　南京市档案馆
尺寸　长 90 厘米　宽 108 厘米

Name　The mental composition of grape pattern brocade
Years　1960s
Collection　Nanjing Archives
Size　Length: 90 cm　Width: 108 cm

The tablecloth mental composition is customized by Nanjing Zhongxingyuan Silk-weaving Factory in the 1960s for Czech Republic.The pattern design is realistic. Through the processing of drawing techniques, the light and shadow effects on grapes and leaves can be vividly expressed.

云锦单色库缎类意匠稿，主体纹样为大洋花，构图丰满，线条流畅柔美。

大洋花纹样早在清代就已出现，为东西方文化交融的见证实例。

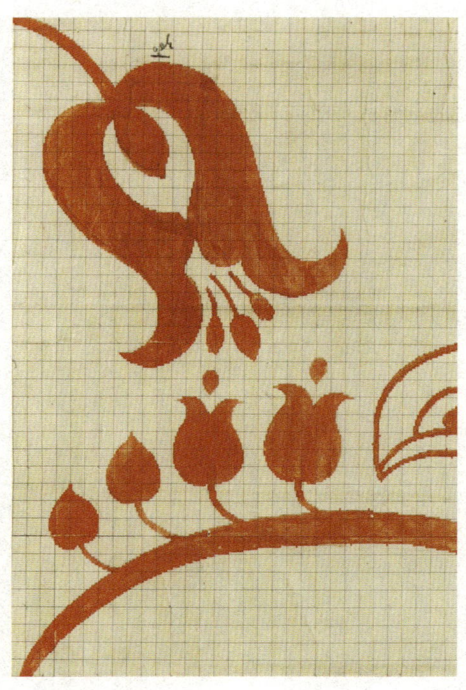

名称　大洋花纹库缎意匠稿
年代　1975 年
收藏　南京市档案馆
尺寸　长 153 厘米　宽 124 厘米

Name　The mental composition of Dayang flower pattern ku satin
Years　1975
Collection　Nanjing Archives
Size　Length: 153 cm　Width: 124 cm

The mental composition is a monochrome satin of Yunjin brocade. The main pattern is Dayang flower. The design is rich and the lines are smooth. Dayang flower appeared duing the Qing Dynasty, which is a witness to the integration of Eastern and Western cultures.

云锦单色库缎类意匠稿，图案设计引入了大洋花和佩兹利纹，佩兹利纹起源于波斯和印度地区，是当地妇女头巾的装饰花纹，后来又流行于欧洲及世界各地，按照此稿生产的面料是南京中兴源丝织厂的外销产品。

佩兹利纹

名称　佩兹利纹库缎意匠稿
年代　1975 年
收藏　南京市档案馆
尺寸　长 170cm　宽 122cm

Name　The mental composition of Paisley pattern ku satin
Years　1975
Collection　Nanjing Archives
Size　Length: 170 cm　Width: 122 cm

The mental composition is a monochrome satin of Yunjin brocade. The pattern design introduces the Dayang flower and Paisley pattern, which is originated in Persia and India. It is the decorative pattern of local women's headscarves, which later became popular in Europe and around the world. It is an export variety of Nanjing Zhongxingyuan Silk-weaving Factory.

该作品图案为满地的布局，四方连续，色彩丰富，线条流畅灵动，一改中国传统图案设计风格，积极吸纳异域图案元素，成为南京中兴源丝织厂生产的民族特需商品之一。

名称　异域花卉纹风华锦实物及意匠稿

年代　1989 年

收藏　南京市档案馆

尺寸　长 70 厘米　宽 81 厘米

Name　The product and the mental composition of exotic flower pattern fenghua brocade

Years　1989

Collection　Nanjing Archives

Size　Length: 70 cm　Width: 81 cm

The brocade is a full layout, continuous in all directions, rich in colors, which display smooth and flexible lines. It changes the traditional Chinese design style of patterns, and actively absorbs exotic elements of patterns. It is a special commodity intended for ethnical use produced by Nanjing Zhongxingyuan Silk textile Factory.

彩库锦是通梭织彩，分段换色，且金线贯穿始终的一种重纬织锦。

它用色虽不多，但织品效果甚为精丽悦目，为常见机织品种。

图示为南京中兴源丝织厂生产的黑地朵花纹彩库锦。

名称　黑地朵花纹彩库锦
年代　1960 年代
收藏　南京市档案馆
尺寸　长 74 厘米　宽 75 厘米

Name　Flower pattern caiku brocade with black ground
Years　1960s
Collection　Nanjing Archives
Size　Length: 74 cm　Width: 75 cm

Caiku brocade is double weft brocade that weaves colors by shuttle. It changes colors by sections, and runs through gold thread.

Although there are not many colors, the effect of the fabric is very beautiful and pleasing to the eye. It is a common woven variety.

The picture shows the black ground multi-flower pattern color Caiku brocade produced by Nanjing Zhongxingyuan Silk-weaving Factory.

凹凸锦是中华人民共和国成立以后开发的创新品种，纬丝用料极粗，故面料厚实，花纹立体感强。

「湖蓝地缠枝牡丹纹凹凸锦」是在湖蓝地上织单色缠枝牡丹纹，黄蓝配色对比强烈。牡丹纹上下两排花头相对为一个循环，缠枝连接相邻花朵，形成四方连续图案。

名称　湖蓝地缠枝牡丹纹凹凸锦
年代　1972 年
收藏　南京市档案馆
尺寸　长 750 厘米　宽 78 厘米

Name　Entangled branch peony pattern rugged brocade with lake blue ground
Years　1972
Collection　Nanjing Archives
Size　Length: 750 cm Width: 78 cm

Rugged brocade is an innovative variety developed since the establishment of the PRC. The weft silk is very thick, so the fabric is thick and the pattern has a strong three-dimensional sense.

The brocade is a monochrome tangled peony pattern woven on the lake blue ground, which has a strong contrast between yellow and blue colors.

The upper and lower rows of flower heads of the peony pattern are opposite to each other in a cycle, and the intertwined branches connect the adjacent flowers to form a continuous pattern in four directions.

金边绸是一种现代机器织造的提花品种，大面积用金，金线为合成金皮线，地纬线常用粘胶丝代替蚕丝，产量高，多用于民族服装镶边。

图示为南京中兴源丝织厂生产的红地菱格纹金边绸。该产品曾荣获『南京市信得过产品』称号。

名称　红地菱格纹金边绸

年代　1980 年代

收藏　南京市档案馆

尺寸　长 108 厘米　宽 75 厘米

Name　Diamond lattice pattern brocade rimmed by gold threads with red ground

Years　1980s

Collection　Nanjing Archives

Size　Length: 108 cm　Width: 75 cm

Gold edged silk is a jacquard variety woven by modern machines. It uses a large amount of synthetic gold leather thread. Viscose is often used to replace silk in ground weft threads, and is mostly used for border trimming of national clothing.

The picture shows the diamond lattice pattern gold edged silk with red ground produced by Nanjing Zhongxingyuan Silk-weaving Factory. The product won the award of "Nanjing Trustworthy Award".

留香绉是用桑蚕丝和有光粘胶人造丝制织的平纹绉地经起花的生织丝绸，又称重经绉。

其主要特点是绸面绉地，色光柔和，呈水浪型织纹，经面缎花的花纹饱满而光泽明亮。

主要用途是做妇女服装面料。

图示为南京中兴源丝织厂绘制的折枝花卉纹留香绉意匠稿。

名称　折枝花卉纹留香绉意匠稿

年代　1961 年

收藏　南京市档案馆

尺寸　长 102 厘米　宽 73 厘米

Name　The mental composition of twisted branch and flower pattern liuxiang crepe

Years　1961

Collection　Nanjing Archives

Size　Length: 102 cm Width: 73 cm

Liuxiang crepe is a plain crepe made of silk and glossy viscose rayon. It is a raw silk with flowered ground.

Its main features are silk surface crepe, soft color and water wave, the satin pattern on the surface is full and bright.

It is mainly used to make women's clothing fabrics.

The picture shows the mental composition of twisted branch and flower pattern Liuxiang crepe drawn by Nanjing Zhongxingyuan Silk-weaving Factory.

金玉缎是一种桑蚕丝和粘胶人造丝色织提花缎类丝织物。

常见纹样为小型朵花满地散点排列，多用于服饰面料。

图示为南京中兴源丝织厂绘制的菊花纹金玉缎意匠稿。

该产品曾荣获『江苏省优良产品』『南京市信得过产品』称号。

名称　菊花纹金玉缎意匠稿
年代　1970 年代
收藏　南京市档案馆
尺寸　长 101 厘米　宽 80 厘米

Name　The mental composition of chrysanthemum pattern jinyu brocade
Years　1970s
Collection　Nanjing Archives
Size　Length: 101 cm　Width: 80 cm

Jinyu satin is a kind of jacquard satin silk fabric by silk and viscose rayon.

The common pattern is a scattered arrangement of small flowers, which is mostly used for clothing fabrics.

The picture shows jinyu satin mental composition drawn by Nanjing Zhongxingyuan Silk-weaving Factory.

The product won the award of "Jiangsu Excellent Product" and "Nanjing Trustworthy Product".

绉是丝绸品种之一，用合股丝线作经，两种不同捻向的强捻丝线作纬，以平纹组织织造而成，分为素织和提花两种，提花品种更为高端。

图示为南京中兴源丝织厂绘制的仿木纹提花绉意匠稿。

Name   The mental composition in imitation of wood texture jacquard crepe
Years   1984
Collection   Nanjing Archives
Size   Length: 53 cm Width: 102 cm

名称　仿木纹提花绸意匠稿
年代　1984 年
收藏　南京市档案馆
尺寸　长 53 厘米　宽 102 厘米

Crepe is one of the silk varieties. The warp yarn is made of silk yarns which are twisted into strands, while the weft yarn is made of silk yarns twisted in opposite directions. This kind of brocade is woven by means of flat pattern weaving. It can be divided into plain weave and jacquard. The jacquard varieties are high-end.

The picture shows a jacquard crepe in imitation of wood made by Nanjing Zhongxingyuan Silk-weaving Factory.

克利缎是一种用桑蚕丝作经，多彩人造丝作纬的提花缎类丝织物，纹样多为中型写实花卉或动物图案，多用于服饰面料。

图示为南京中兴源丝织厂绘制的团龙纹克利缎意匠稿。

该产品曾荣获『江苏省优良产品』『南京市信得过产品』称号。

名称　团龙纹克利缎意匠稿
年代　1980 年代
收藏　南京市档案馆
尺寸　直径 76 厘米

Name　The mental composition of group dragon pattern Kelly satin
Years　1980s
Collection　Nanjing Archives
Size　Diameter: 76 cm

Kelly satin is a kind of jacquard satin silk fabric with silk as warp and colorful rayon as weft. The patterns are mostly medium-sized realistic flower or animal patterns. It is mostly used for clothing fabrics.

The picture shows a Kelly satin painted by Nanjing Zhongxingyuan Silk-weaving Factory.

The product won the award of "Jiangsu Excellent Product" and "Nanjing Trustworthy Product".

该意匠稿描绘了两只仙鹤纤细灵动，飞翔在桃树和松树之间，布局协调柔和。仙鹤、松树、寿桃均为中国传统祝寿题材，表达人们对长寿和幸福生活的向往。

名称　松鹤寿桃纹织锦缎意匠稿
年代　1940 年
收藏　南京市档案馆
尺寸　长 230 厘米　宽 110 厘米

Name　The mental composition of pine crane and peach pattern zhuanghua satin
Years　1940
Collection　Nanjing Archives
Size　Length: 230 cm　Width: 110 cm

The brocade depicts two cranes, delicate and flexible, flying between peach trees and pine trees. The layout is harmonious and soft.

Cranes, pine trees and peaches are all symbols of traditional Chinese birthday greetings, which express the yearning for longevity and happiness.

该意匠稿根据于非闇画作绘制，由五只不同颜色的鸽子及四角的祥云组成，表达祝愿和平之意。

该意匠稿右下角注有『祥辉瑞霭照耀和平／于非闇六十四岁作』的字样及印章。

祥輝瑞靄晱燿和平
于北闇六十歲作

名称　和平鸽织锦缎意匠稿
年代　1962 年
收藏　南京市档案馆
尺寸　长 224 厘米　宽 135 厘米

Name　The mental composition of peace dove woven brocade
Years　1962
Collection　Nanjing Archives
Size　Length: 224 cm Width: 135 cm

The brocade is painted according to the work of Yu Feiyin. It depicts five pigeons with different colors and auspicious clouds at four corners to express the wish for peace.

The lower right corner of the mental composition is marked with the seal "auspicious light shines on peach/made at the age of 64 by Yu Feiyin".

该意匠稿由莲花、宝相花、如意头、连钱纹等元素构成。

天华锦的设计通常是规矩的几何框架，中间饰以满地花朵，且几何框架构成八个方向，有『四通八达』之意，织造时根据配色不同，可华丽亦可朴素。

天华锦又名『添花锦』，取其『锦上添花』之意。

名称　莲花纹天华锦意匠稿
年代　1976 年
收藏　南京市档案馆
尺寸　长 100 厘米　宽 90 厘米

Name　The mental composition of lotus pattern Tianhua Brocade
Years　1976
Collection　Nanjing Archives
Size　Length: 100 cm　Width: 90 cm

The mental composition of this brocade embodies such elements as lotus, baoxiang flower, ruyi head, lianqian pattern and so on.

It is usually a regular geometric frame, with flowers in the middle, and forms eight directions, which indicates "extending in all directions", weaving can be either gorgeous or simplistic according to the requirements for matching the colors.

The Tianhua brocade is associated with Chinese characters "tianhuajin", bearning the meaning of "adding luster to something".

该意匠稿单位图案主体为双龙纹，一条昂首振尾向上（升龙），一条俯身向下（降龙），龙身周围藏八宝环绕，符合云锦花清地白、锦空匀齐的图案设计技巧，画面充满吉祥之意。

名称　云龙八吉祥织锦缎意匠稿
年代　1988 年
收藏　南京市档案馆
尺寸　长 160 厘米　宽 100 厘米

Name　The mental composition of cloud dragon and eight treasures' brocade
Years　1988
Collection　Nanjing Archives
Size　Length: 160 cm Width: 100 cm

The main body of the brocade pattern is two dragons. One dragon is holding up the head and wagging its tail in the sky, while the other is bending down. The dragon body is surrounded by eight treasures, which conform to the designing techniques of Yunjin brocade that patterns ought to be clear-cut, the ground ought to be orderly, and the spatial layout is arranged evenly and uniformly. The brocade is full of auspicious meaning.

该意匠稿团花部分描绘五只蝙蝠围绕寿字，寓意「五福捧寿」，另有「寿」字设计成不同字体，意为多寿，分布在五蝠周围。云锦吉祥图案常取纹样的谐音，蝠谐音为「福」，该纹样为中国传统祝寿题材。

名称　福寿纹织锦缎意匠稿
年代　1988 年
收藏　南京市档案馆
尺寸　长 118 厘米　宽 82 厘米

Name   The mental composition of blessing and longevity pattern woven brocade
Years   1988
Collection   Nanjing Archives
Size   Length: 118 cm Width: 82 cm

The pattern of the brocade depicts five bats surrounding the word "寿 (shou)", which means blessing and longevity. In addition, the word "寿 (shou)" is designed into different fonts around the five bats, which indicates more longevity.

The auspicious patterns of Yunjin brocade often take homophones, as the homophone of bat is "福 (fu)" in Chinese, the pattern features a traditional Chinese birthday celebration theme.

该设计稿选取暗八仙中的四个法器为设计元素，将吉祥寓意的暗八仙图案和蝴蝶纹巧妙结合，古朴典雅、锦空匀称。

根据记载，此图示纹样作者为云锦老艺人张福永。

八仙
吉庆之意.
椅垫
晚清四十年（1854年记）

来源、创制
作者：倪福永.
存样处：中央院.

八A1.

备注：销洋装. 四合椅垫.
此号草稿不完全.

名称　暗八仙手绘设计稿
年代　1954 年
收藏　正源兴绸缎庄
尺寸　长 39 厘米　宽 27 厘米

Name　The "Hint Eight Immortals" hand-painted design mental draft
Years　1954
Collection　Cheng Yuan Hsing Co., Ltd.
Size　Length: 39 cm　Width: 27 cm

The "Hint eight immortals" hand-painted design mental composition selects four magic instruments in the Hint eight immortals as design elements. The design ingeniously combines the Hint eight immortals pattern with the butterfly pattern, which is auspicious, simple and elegant, and the brocade is symmetrical. The picture shows the hand-painted design of the Hint eight immortals.

According to records, the pattern is written by an old artist of Yunjin brocade named Zhang Fuyong.

该设计稿图案来源于清末正源兴绸缎庄经典作品。

凤戏牡丹为吉庆之意，专为库缎品种设计可织成暗花缎或闪缎。

图示为一九六二年云锦老艺人王道惠绘制的凤戏牡丹富贵长春图设计稿。

距今七八十年前.
八团花袍料纹
推磨擘剖摆,
双凤呈祥、鸳
子富贵五福门
十封托连续

祥云流

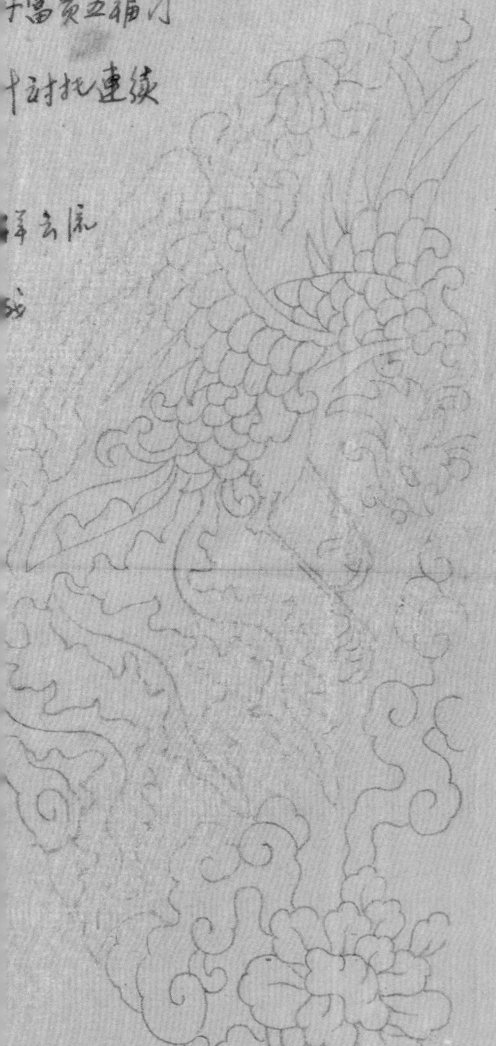

牡36.

牡33.

富贵长春、吉祥云气、库缎(二则)

(富贵光长春地)

花纹审慎,沿光空白二分处惠曲折

长春地,擘破光对头颠倒摆。牡丹花

二合对束,中心花头上下沿光边改二花叶

成一花二叶之团光。

王道惠

1962.2.13.

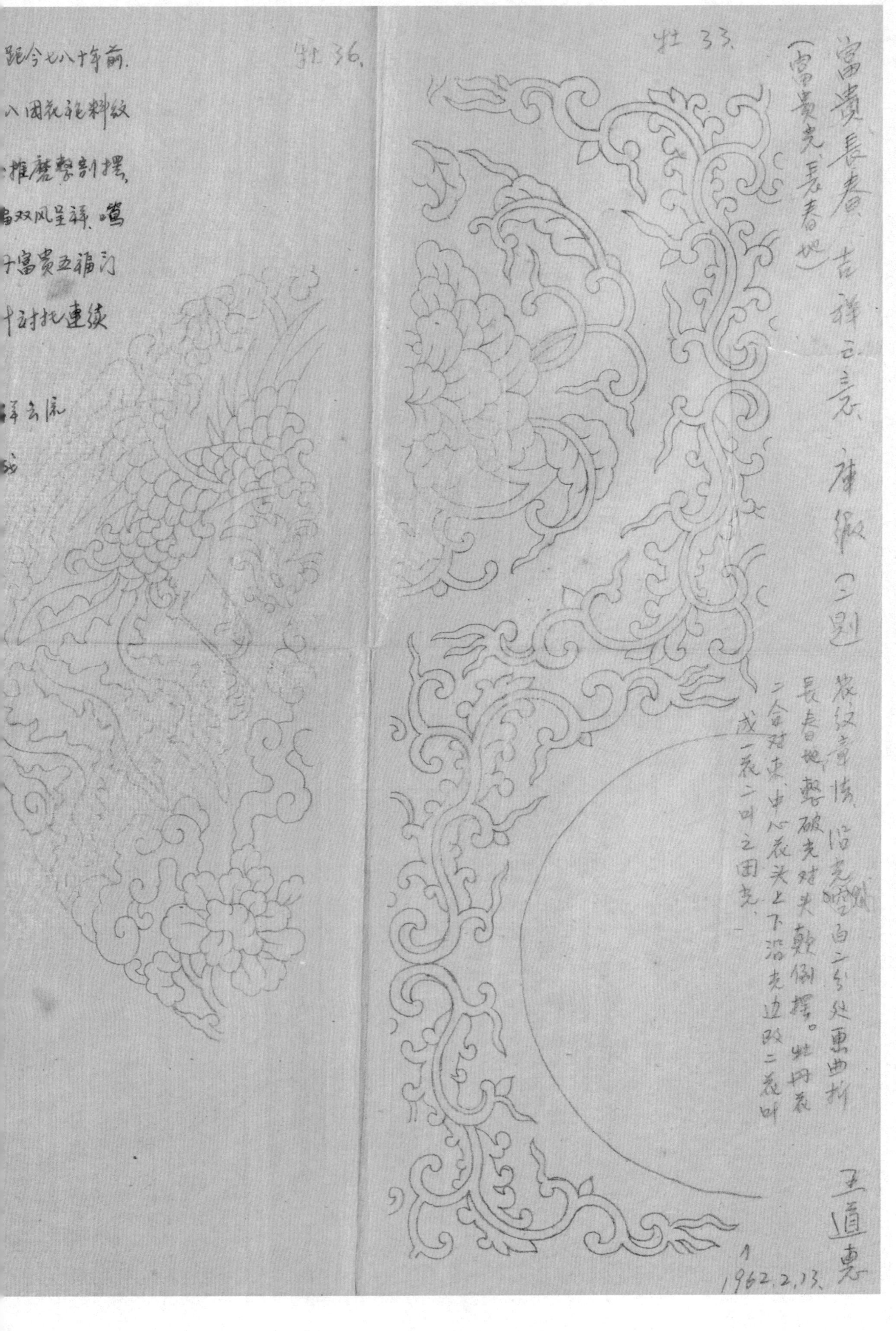

名称　凤戏牡丹富贵长春图手绘设计稿

年代　1962 年

收藏　正源兴绸缎庄

尺寸　长 31.5 厘米　宽 28 厘米

Name　The hand-painted design mental draft of phoenix playing with peony, prosperity and longevity

Years　1962

Collection　Cheng Yuan Hsing Co., Ltd.

Size　Length: 31.5 cm　Width: 28 cm

The pattern comes from one of the classic works of Cheng Yuan Hsing Co., Ltd. in the late Qing Dynasty.

The pattern of phoenix playing with peony implies auspice, it is specially designed for the variety of ku satin, and it can be woven into hidden flower satin or flash satin.

The picture shows the design draft of "The hand-painted design mental draft of phoenix playing with peony, prosperity and longevity" by an old Yunjin brocade artist Wang Daohui in 1962.

该设计稿融合传统，以卍字底纹，搭配折枝「梅兰竹菊」四君子，寓意吉祥、高雅。

图案巧妙采用「四方连续，八面接章」的设计理念，单位循环连续，

富有一种错落有致、层次分明、和谐平衡的美感。

王道襄
1963.9.24.

名称　卐字纹梅兰竹菊手绘设计稿
年代　1963 年
收藏　正源兴绸缎庄
尺寸　长 30 厘米　宽 16.5 厘米

Name　The hand-painted design mental draft of 卐 pattern with plum, orchid, bamboo and chrysanthemum
Years　1963
Collection　Cheng Yuan Hsing Co., Ltd.
Size　Length: 30 cm　Width: 16.5 cm

The design integrates traditions. 中 is used as its background and four gentle things of "plum, orchid, bamboo and chrysanthemum" are adorned with twisted branches and flowers, implying auspiciousness and elegance.

The pattern ingeniously adopts the design concept of "four directions are continuous, eight sides are connected", and the unit cycle is continuous, which conveys clear-cut layers, harmony and balance.

该作品为复制定陵博物馆出土妆花纱文物所绘。

该纹样为四方连续图案，『整剖光』结构。

意匠稿巧妙运用局部替换的方式将阴阳双鱼纹和团鹤纹灵活转换，提高了意匠工作的效率。

妆花纱是云锦中织造难度较高的品种，是在真丝绞纱组织上装饰五彩花纹，兔纹用金线织出，配以彩纬挖织双鱼纹和团鹤纹，再现明代妆花工艺成就。

名称　织金奔兔衔灵芝纹妆花纱手绘设计稿和意匠稿

年代　1970 年代

收藏　正源兴绸缎庄

尺寸　长 37 厘米　宽 40 厘米 / 长 59 厘米　宽 36 厘米

Name　The hand-painted design mental draft and the mental composition of running rabbit woven
　　　with gold thread grasping ganoderma pattern zhuanghua satin with gold thread

Years　1970s

Collection　Cheng Yuan Hsing Co., Ltd.

Size　Length: 37 cm　Width: 40 cm / Length: 59 cm　Width: 36 cm

The mental composition is drawn in order to replicate the cultural relics of zhuanghua yarn from Dingling Museum.

The pattern is a continuous pattern on four sides, with a "zhengpouguang" structure.

The ingenious use of partial replacement in the design flexibly converts the yin-yang double fish pattern and the crane pattern, which improves the efficiency of the artist.

Zhuanghua yarn is a kind of brocade with high weaving difficulty. It is decorated with colorful patterns on the silk twisted yarn. The rabbit pattern is woven with gold threads, in harmony with double fish and crane patterns woven by colored wefts. It embodies the achievements of the zhuanghua craft of the Ming Dynasty.

该手绘设计稿将暗八仙元素应用于云锦图案设计中，古朴典雅。暗八仙得名于八仙所持法器，暗指八位仙人，纹样寓意吉祥。篆体寿字与如意祥云组成祝寿之意。

织只 云地八仙金篆寿 金花缎拼
八 A8
云锦图案手抄研究资
抄 P2
1986.11.3. 惠

名称　云地暗八仙金篆寿字纹手绘设计稿

年代　1986 年

收藏　正源兴绸缎庄

尺寸　长 35 厘米　宽 31 厘米

Name　The hand-painted design mental draft of the Hint Eight Immortals and golden
　　　" 寿 (Shou)" with cloud ground

Years　1986

Collection　Cheng Yuan Hsing Co., Ltd.

Size　Length: 35 cm　Width: 31 cm

The mental composition applies the Hint eight immortals element to the pattern design of Yunjin brocade, which is simple and elegant.

The Hint eight immortals are named after the magic tools held by the eight immortals, which imply immortality. The patterns imply auspiciousness.

The seal character " 寿 (Shou)" and "Ruyi auspicious cloud" constitute the meaning of birthday celebration.

二色织金锦是一种地纬织于织物背面，表面用金、银两种质地的线织成的提花织物。

小花纹内的圆金和圆银线配色光泽和谐，显高贵且文雅的艺术特征。

此意匠纸为南京中兴源丝织厂创制，背面详细记载了织机装造参数。

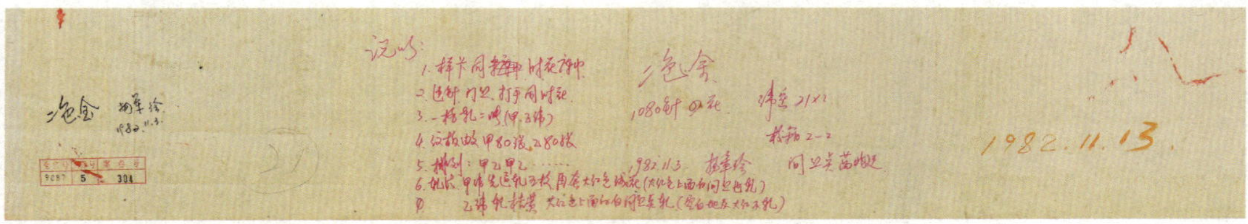

Name   The mental composition of geometric flower pattern brocade woven with gold threads by two colors
Years   1982
Collection   Nanjing Archives
Size   Length: 22 cm Width: 83 cm

名称　几何花卉纹二色织金锦意匠稿
年代　1982 年
收藏　南京市档案馆
尺寸　长 22 厘米　宽 83 厘米

"Two colors weaving gold brocade" is a jacquard fabric woven with ground weft on the back of the fabric and gold and silver thread on the surface.

The round gold and silver threads in the small pattern are harmonious in color and luster, showing noble and elegant artistic features.

The picture shows the two-color gold brocade drawn by Nanjing Zhongxingyuan Silk-weaving Factory and the back of mental composition records the loom installation parameters in detail.

　　以云锦为代表的丝织业在古都南京这片人文荟萃的沃土上世代相传，连绵相继。二十世纪八十年代，南京中兴源丝织厂进入鼎盛时期，产品种类丰富，不少品种获得国家、省、市级奖项，如该厂著名的"松鹤牌"云锦，曾荣获国家质量银质奖、纺织工业部名牌产品、纺织工业部优质产品奖；花软缎、素软缎、双绉获省优良产品奖。南京中兴源丝织厂这批云锦实物档案被南京市档案馆收藏，成为南京工业遗产档案的重要组成部分。

　　2009年9月30日南京云锦成功申遗，是对历代云锦工匠的认可，是对云锦产业取得成就的认可，更是对南京云锦文化传承的认可，这是政府、行业、全社会共同努力的成果。

　　近年来，以档案馆、博物馆为代表的专业机构正在尝试运用现代化手段保护传承云锦，以科技助力传统文化，扎实开展研究工作，云锦的社会化保护平台逐渐形成，为新时代背景下传统文化的继承和发展开辟了新道路。

　　自2019年起，南京市档案馆、南京江南丝绸文化博物馆等开展了一系列云锦保护传承项目，取得了"南京云锦及丝织业档案活化""云锦数字化保护"等创新成果，开启现代化保护的新篇章。

Enchanting Scent of Spring

The silk industry, of which Nanjing Yunjin brocade is a typical example, is descended from one generation to another in Nanjing, an ancient capital where talents are clustered. In the 1980s, Nanjing Zhongxingyuan Silk-manufacturing Factory reached its heyday, when the diversified categories of products reaped many awards by the national, provincial and municipal government. These archives are preserved in the Nanjing Archives, which are integral to the archives of Nanjing industrial legacy.

On September 30, 2009, the Nanjing Yunjin brocade succeeded in applying for the world's intangible cultural heritage, which was a recognition of the brocade craftsmen over the centuries, the achievements of the brocade industry and the inheritance of Nanjing Yunjin brocade culture. It was the joint efforts made by the government, industry and society that gave rise to this honor.

The professional organs such as archival center and museums are striving to protect the Nanjing Yunjin brocade and disseminate the culture by modern means against the backdrop of the New Era. With the platform for protecting the Nanjing Yunjin brocade on a social level formed, science and technology are giving impetus to traditional culture, while researches into Nanjing Yunjin brocade are steadily carried out. Such measures taken pave the way for preserving and inheriting traditional culture in the New Era.

Since 2019, Nanjing Archives and Nanjing Jiangnan Silk Culture Museum have carried out a series of projects intended to protect and inherit Nanjing Yunjin brocade, and have accomplished such results of innovation as "The Activation of Nanjing Yunjin Brocade and Silk Industry" and "The Digitalized Protection of Nanjing Yunjin Brocade", which ushers in a new episode for modern protection.

该作品纹饰源自清代皇家贺寿经典图案，主要由狮子和杂宝纹组成，绣球居于中间，周围杂宝环绕，整剖光结构。

设计活泼灵动，呈现一派喜庆欢快之气。

此作品的三套配色样品保存完好，是南京中兴源丝织厂热销产品，受到市场欢迎。

名称　狮子盘球意匠稿及实物
年代　1974 年
收藏　南京市档案馆
尺寸　长 220 厘米　宽 110 厘米

Name　The mental composition and the product of lion dribbling
Years　1974
Collection　Nanjing Archives
Size　Length: 220 cm　Width: 110 cm

狮子盘球成品图

The "lion ball" pattern is derived from the classic pattern of royal birthday celebrations in the Qing Dynasty, it is mainly composed of lion and miscellaneous treasure patterns, the embroidered ball is in the middle, surrounded by miscellaneous treasures, and has a zhengpouguang structure.

The design is lively and vivid, presenting a festive atmosphere.

The three sets of the color for the samples are well preserved. They are most popular products of Nanjing Zhongxingyuan Silk-weaving Factory and are popular in the market.

该意匠稿图案为缠枝莲花纹，莲花大小不一，形态各异，线条流畅，满地四方连续的设计，使画面丰富且有韵律。

风华锦是多彩提花织物，该产品曾荣获国家经济委员会『优秀新产品（金龙奖）』。

名称　富贵莲花纹风华锦意匠稿
年代　1982 年
收藏　南京市档案馆
尺寸　长 83 厘米　宽 85 厘米

Name　The mental composition of prosperity lotus pattern fenghua brocade
Years　1982
Collection　Nanjing Archives
Size　Length: 83 cm　Width: 85 cm

The pattern of the brocade is a tangled lotus. The lotus flowers are of different sizes and shapes. The lines are smooth and continuous. The picture is rich and rhythmic.

This brocade is a colorful jacquard fabric and has won the awards of "Excellent New Product (Golden Dragon Award)" from National Economic Commission.

福禄锦图案由牡丹、佛手、铜钱、石榴组成，象征幸福美满之意。此产品当时定向销往西藏地区，色彩依据藏族传统文化的五色而配，蓝、白、红、黄、绿分别代表天、云、火、土、水。南京中兴源丝织厂生产的福禄锦曾荣获「江苏省优秀产品（金牛奖）」。

Name   The mental composition and the product of fulu brocade
Years   1986
Collection   Nanjing Archives
Size   Length: 144 cm Width: 99 cm

名称　福禄锦意匠稿及实物
年代　1986 年
收藏　南京市档案馆
尺寸　长 144 厘米　宽 99 厘米

The pattern of Fulu brocade is composed of peony, bergamot, copper coin and pomegranate, which symbolizes happiness.

This product was sold to Tibet directionally. The color was matched according to the five colors of Tibetan traditional culture, blue, white, red, yellow and green represent sky, cloud, fire, earth and water, respectively.

Fulu brocade produced by Nanjing Zhongxingyuan Silk-weaving Factory has won "High Quality Product Award of Jiangsu Province (Gold Bull Award)".

金陵锦是南京中兴源丝织厂的原创产品，面料主体花纹为莲花和牡丹，缠枝连接各个花头，中间饰佛教八宝图案，寓意「吉庆富贵、福禄万代」。花纹为上下交错横向排列，四排一循环，面料配色丰富，以二晕色展现花朵的层次感。南京市档案馆保存有完整的意匠稿和机织面料原件，后用云锦木机大花楼织机对此档案进行复原，并根据手工妆花织造方法进行再配色。

原件   复原件

Name   Jinling brocade
Years   1989
Collection   Nanjing Archives
Size   Length: 237 cm Width: 78 cm

意匠稿原件

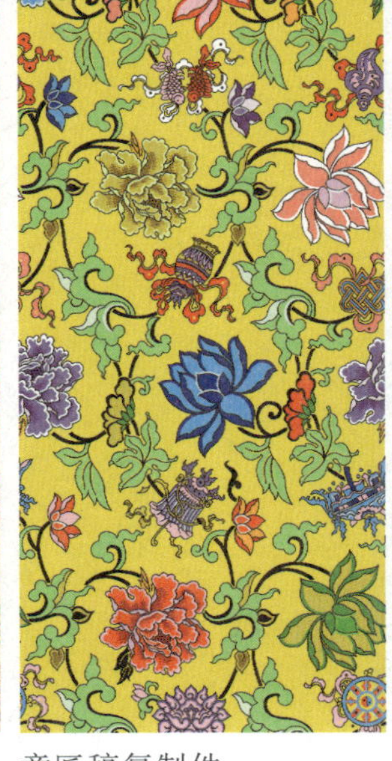

意匠稿复制件

细节图

名称　金陵锦

年代　1989 年

收藏　南京市档案馆

尺寸　长 237 厘米　宽 78 厘米

Jinling brocade is an original product of Nanjing Zhongxingyuan Silk-weaving Factory, the main pattern of the fabric is features lotus and peony, with intertwined branches connecting each flower's head. The middle is decorated with the eight treasures pattern of Buddhism, which means auspice, richness and nobility, and prosperity for later generations.

The pattern is staggered horizontally from top to bottom, with four rows as one cycle. The fabric is rich in color, showing the layering feeling of flowers in two halos.

The Nanjing Archives has kept a complete manuscript of the artist and the original woven fabric. Later, the archives were restored by Yunjin brocade wood loom and dahualou loom, and the colors were re-matched according to the zhuanghua skills.

该面料根据定陵出土袍料复制。

在红色绞纱地上通织平纹暗花纹，并用妆花技法织团纹，纱地暗花由云纹构成，妆花团纹由行龙纹组成。

原料由多规格真丝线、孔雀羽线、圆真金线等珍贵材料组成。

名称　明·万历 红地无极灵芝云纹织金孔雀羽妆花纱团龙袍料（复制品）
年代　1983 年
收藏　江宁织造博物馆
尺寸　长 1750 厘米　宽 68 厘米

Name　The imperial robe materials decorated with clusters of dragons, featuring ganoderma, cloud pattern, peacock feather woven with gold threads zhuanghua yarn with red ground (Emperor Wanli, Ming Dynasty) (replica)
Years　1983
Collection　Jiangning Imperial Silk-manufacturing Museum
Size　Length: 1750 cm Width: 68 cm

The brocade is a replicate of the robe materials excavated from Dingling tomb.

Plain hidden flower pattern is woven on the red twisted yarn ground, and the clustering pattern is woven by zhuanghua techniques. The hidden flower on the yarn ground is composed of cloud pattern, and the mental composition clustering pattern is composed of dragon pattern.

The raw materials are composed of real silk thread in various calibers, peacock feather thread, round gold thread and other precious materials.

该龙袍原件现藏于北京故宫博物院，圆领、右衽、马蹄袖、大摆、四开裾，为清代龙袍典型的型制。

龙袍通身以云锦妆花工艺织造而成。

古代帝王有『九五之尊』之称，因此龙袍共有九条五爪金龙。

龙袍下摆斜向排列着许多弯曲的线条，名谓『水脚』。

水脚之上，还有许多波浪翻滚的水浪，水浪之上，又立有山石宝物，

它除了表示绵延不断的吉祥含义之外，还有『一统山河』和『万世升平』的寓意。

名称　清·雍正 黄地五彩云龙妆花缎龙袍（复制品）
年代　2019 年
收藏　南京江南丝绸文化博物馆
尺寸　衣长 144 厘米　二袖通长 190 厘米　下摆宽 130 厘米

Name　The imperial robe of colorful cloud and dragon zhuanghua satin with yellow ground (Emperor Yongzheng, Qing Dynasty) (replica)
Years　2019
Collection　Nanjing Jiangnan Silk Culture Museum
Size　Length: 144cm, Length of Two Sleeves 190cm, Width of Lower Hem 130 cm

The original brocade is preserved in the Palace Museum in Beijing. It has a round neck, a right lapel, horseshoe sleeves, a large pendant, and four open trains. It is typical of Dragon Robe in the Qing Dynasty.

The Dragon Robe is woven with Yunjin brocade weaving and zhuanghua techniques.

The ancient emperors were known as "the royal supremacy". Therefore, the Dragon Robe had nine golden dragons with five claws. Many curved lines are arranged obliquely at the lap of the Dragon Robe, which is called "water feet".

On the water feet, there are many rolling water waves. On the water waves, there are also mountains and stones. In addition to the auspicious meaning of continuity and endurance, it also implies dominance over mountains and rivers and eternal peace.

该凤袍原件收藏于北京故宫博物院，为乾隆时期皇后春秋季所穿吉服。

香黄色妆花缎面料织有江崖海水及九衔枝翔凤纹，多用扁金线勾边，圆金线妆织八宝纹，

翔凤衔牡丹、海棠、梅花折枝花卉代表富贵、美丽、坚强、福运等含义，凤尾晕色自然，

妆花经纬密度较高，纹样细腻，水纹线条圆润，整体配色丰富而协调。

Name　The phoenix robe of nine flying phoenix, cliff and sea water pattern zhuanghua satin with yellow ground (Emperor Qianlong, Qing Dynasty) (replica)

Years　2021

Collection　Nanjing Jiangnan Silk Culture Museum

Size　Length: 144cm, Length of Two Sleeves 174cm, Width of Lower Hem 124 cm

名称　清·乾隆 香黄地九翔凤江崖海水纹妆花缎凤袍（复制品）

年代　2021 年

收藏　南京江南丝绸文化博物馆

尺寸　衣长 144 厘米 二袖通长 174 厘米 下摆宽 124 厘米

The original brocade is preserved in the Palace Museum in Beijing. It is the auspicious dress worn by the empress during the reign of Qianlong in spring and autumn.

The fragrant yellow mental composition fabric is woven with the pattern of sea water beside the cliffs and nine branches with phoenix, most of which are brimmed with flat gold thread, and the round gold thread is used to weave the Babao pattern. The auspicious phoenix bearing peony, begonia and plum blossoms with twisted plum branches represent wealth, beauty, strength and good luck. The phoenix tail is naturally faint, warp yarn and weft yarn of zhuanghua are massively applied, the pattern is delicate, the water lines are round, and the overall color is rich and coordinated.

云锦大花楼织机是我国古代提花机发展的顶峰，它的特点主要是能够表现大图案、多色彩、组织变化丰富的各类提花织物。纬向纹样宽度可达全幅，甚至可以是拼幅和巨型阔幅。

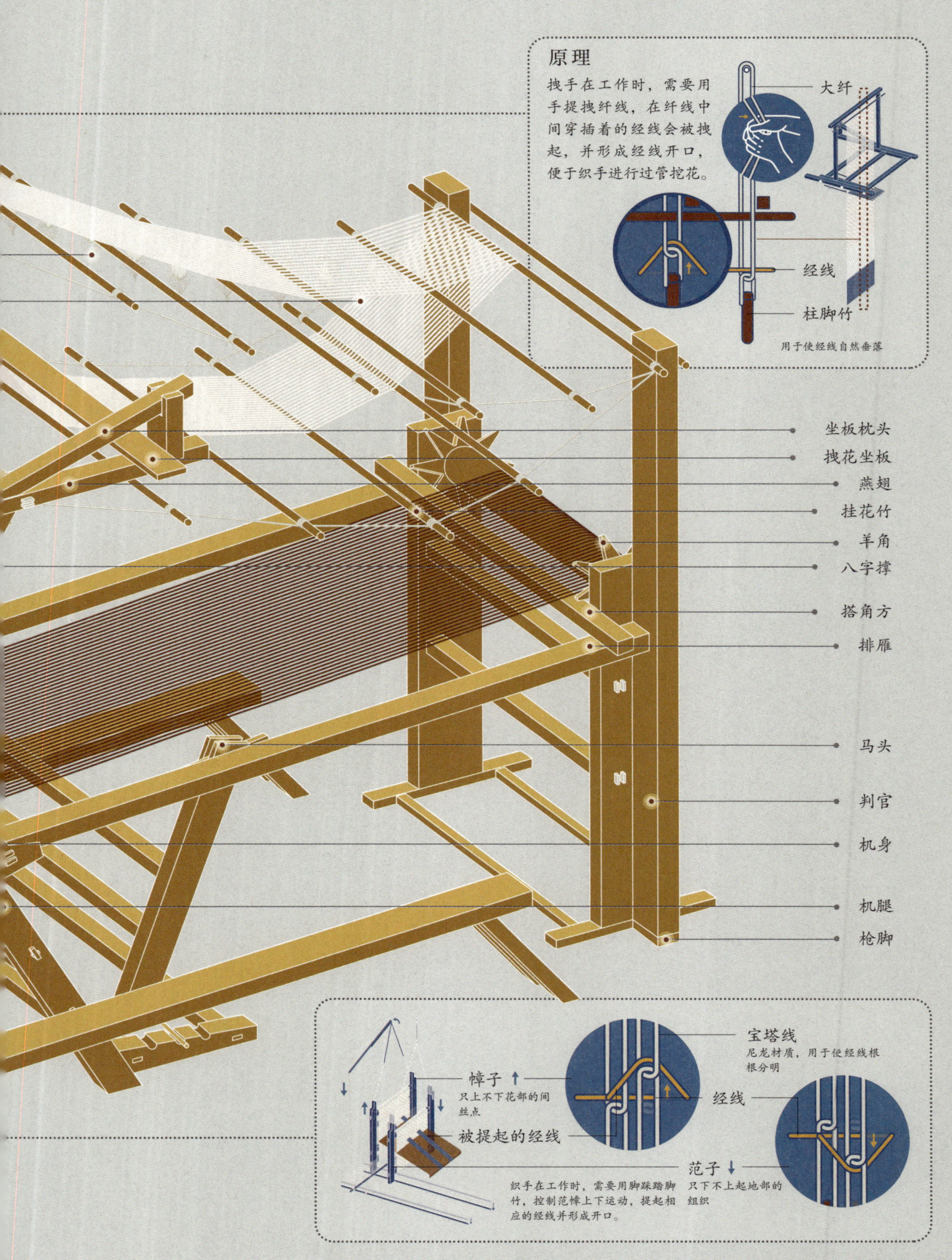

原理
拽手在工作时，需要用手提拽纤线，在纤线中间穿插着的经线会被拽起，并形成经线开口，便于织手进行过管挖花。

大纤
经线
柱脚竹
用于使经线自然垂落

坐板枕头
拽花坐板
燕翅
挂花竹
羊角
八字撑
搭角方
排雁
马头
判官
机身
机腿
枪脚

幛子
只上不下花部的间丝点
被提起的经线
织手在工作时，需要用脚踩踏脚竹，控制范幛上下运动，提起相应的经线并形成开口。

宝塔线
尼龙材质，用于使经线根根分明
经线
范子
只下不上起地部的组织

大花楼织机

沿用古代结绳记事的方式，梳理花本耳子线的同时，也记录了花本与意匠图之间的关系，一个结表示意匠图上的一牙。

冲天盖
千斤筒
大纤
撮
花本

顶梁
三架梁
干出力
过山龙
鸭子嘴
吊蔑
鹦歌架
花门梁
幛子
范子
筘框
局头
拖机布
寸局
柱脚竹
老鼠闩
横沿竹
踏马竹
横档
脚竹

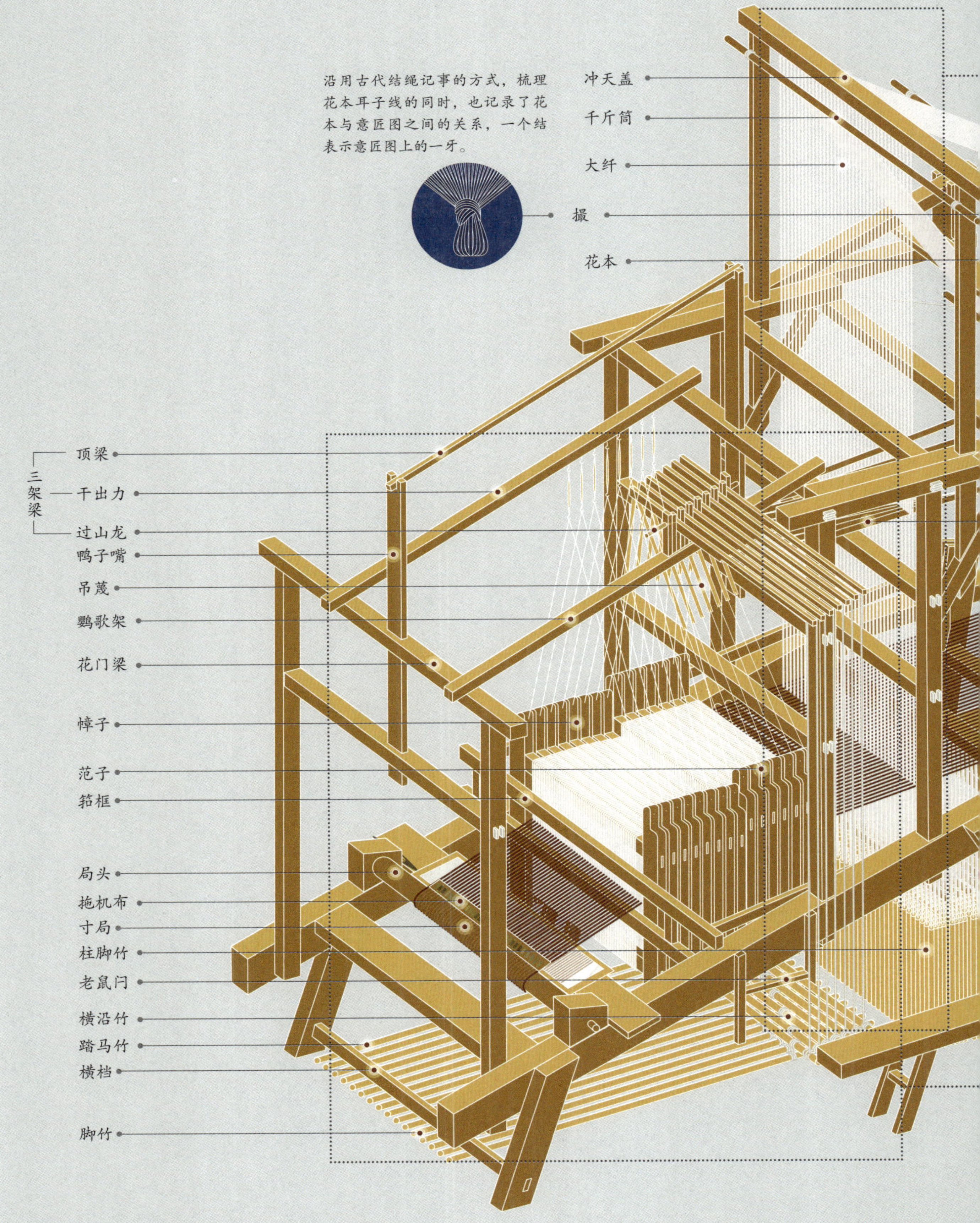

Dahualou loom of Nanjing Yunjin brocade is at the summit of the development history of jacquard. It can display large patterns expressively in multiple colors, and can bring forth a range of jacquard fabrics.

The width of the weft thread can be as long as the length of the whole brocade, and can even reach the length of combined brocades and brocades of larger sizes.

　　以南京云锦为代表的丝织业随着时代进步不断发展，从产业贡献升华到文化滋养，成为一份深刻的城市文化印记。

　　丝织品是物质的，而技艺是无形的；档案和文物是有形的，文化和智慧又是无形的。南京云锦的文物、艺术品、织造技艺、档案史料和文献等，要通过不断发掘、梳理、沉淀、积累才能形成传承不息的云锦文化，才是体现物质与精神整体性的文化遗产，更是新时代文化复兴的宝藏。

　　近年来，南京市档案馆围绕南京云锦非遗档案的开发利用，开展了一系列项目，与南京轻纺产业（集团）有限公司合作完成了中兴源云锦档案的接收进馆；与南京江南丝绸文化博物馆合作，对馆藏的云锦档案资料开展保护活化工作，同时联合南京正源兴服饰设计有限公司举办了档案史料展览；以"南京民族工商业档案开发"为课题申报的国家重点档案保护与开发项目经国家档案局批复立项，使得社会各界有机会一起回顾南京云锦及丝织工业的百年复兴历程，一起感受"织造之府"的深厚底蕴，见证"正本清源·百年中兴"的传承不息，探寻"文化基因"的来龙去脉。人们对南京云锦的研究和认知，也从仅限于织造工艺的研究，提升到中华民族创造能力和智慧结晶的高度。

　　文化遗产的传承保护工作任重而道远，她守护的是中华民族的智慧和技能，是传统文化在不同历史阶段的光辉成就。人有百年，纸存千载，文以载道，生生不息，中国优秀的传统文化必将通过一代代守护者的不懈努力，走向"复兴锦程"的璀璨未来。

　　本书图片由南京鹰联视界文化传媒有限公司拍摄。第一、第二章图片说明由肖妍娜执笔，第三章图片说明由戴萌、肖妍娜执笔、第四章图片说明由陈奕通、肖妍娜执笔。王道惠、戴健、俞征智三位专家作为特聘顾问指导、审阅书稿，付出了辛勤劳动。谨向上述同志致以诚挚的感谢！

The silk-weaving industry represented by Nanjing Yunjin brocade has been developing with the progress of time. In terms of industrial contribution and cultural nourishment, it has left a profound urban cultural imprint.

Silk fabrics are tangible, while technique is not; archives and cultural relics are tangible, while culture and wisdom are not. Cultural relics, works of art, weaving skills, archival historical materials and documents of Nanjing Yunjin brocade, can form a resilient culture through continuous excavation, sorting, and accumulation. It is not only a cultural heritage that reflects the integrity of material and spirit, but also a treasure of cultural renaissance in the New Era.

In recent years, Nanjing Archives has carried out a series of projects concerning the development and utilization of the intangible cultural heritage archives of Nanjing Yunjin brocade. Nanjing Archives, in cooperation with Nanjing Light Textile Industry Co., Ltd. has completed the reception of Zhongxingyuan Yunjin brocade archives; Nanjing Archives has cooperated with Nanjing Jiangnan Silk Culture Museum in the protection and activation of Nanjing Yunjin brocade archives, and at the same time, organized exhibitions of the archives with Nanjing Cheng Yuan Hsing Fashion Design Co., Ltd; Nanjing Archives has applied for a National Key Archives Protection and Development Project, revolving around "Development of Nanjing National Industrial and Commercial Archives", and this application has been approved of by Nation Archives Administration of China. Thus, this project gives all walks of society the opportunity to review the hundred years' rejuvenation process of Nanjing Yunjing brocade and silk-weaving industry, experience the profundity of the weaving bureau, witness the continuous inheritance of the hundred-year history of Zhongxing, and explore the origin of cultural genes. Our research and understanding of Nanjing Yunjin brocade have been advanced from researching into the weaving techniques to improving the creativity and wisdom of the Chinese nation.

The inheritance and protection of cultural heritage have a long way to go. It safeguards the wisdom and skills of our nation and is the brilliant achievements of traditional culture in different historical stages. Humans can hardly live more than 100 years, paper can survive thousands of years, and canons serve as a vehicle to clarify reason and doctrines. China's excellent traditional culture will surely move towards a bright future of rejuvenation through the unremitting efforts of generations of guardians.

The pictures of this book are offered by Nanjing United Eagle Vision Cultural Media Co., Ltd. Chapter I and II are illustrated by Xiao Yanna, Chapter III by Dai Meng and Xiao Yanna, Chapter IV by Chen Yitong and Xiao Yanna. Wang Daohui, Dai Jian and Yu Zhengzhi, as the special consultants, have worked hard to guide and review the manuscript. We express sincere gratitude to the abovementioned comrades.

图书在版编目（CIP）数据

锦冠：南京云锦及丝织业档案图典 / 南京市档案馆编.
-- 南京：南京出版社, 2023.1
ISBN 978-7-5533-3558-2

Ⅰ.①南… Ⅱ.①南… Ⅲ.①织锦缎 – 纺织工业 – 档
案 – 史料 – 南京②丝织物 – 纺织工业 – 档案 – 史料 – 南京
Ⅳ.①F426.81

中国版本图书馆CIP数据核字（2021）第272977号

书　　名	锦冠：南京云锦及丝织业档案图典
编　　者	南京市档案馆
出版发行	南京出版传媒集团
	南京出版社

社址	南京市太平门街53号	邮编	210016
网址	http://www.njcbs.cn	电子信箱	njcbs1988@163.com
联系电话	025-83283893、83283864（营销）	025-83112257（编务）	

出 版 人	项晓宁
出 品 人	卢海鸣
责任编辑	朱天乐　崔龙龙
书籍设计	王　俊
责任印制	杨福彬

排　　版	上海雅昌艺术印刷有限公司
印　　刷	上海雅昌艺术印刷有限公司
开　　本	889毫米×1194毫米　1/16
印　　张	33
字　　数	300千
版　　次	2023年1月第1版
印　　次	2023年1月第1次印刷
书　　号	ISBN 978-7-5533-3558-2
定　　价	498.00元

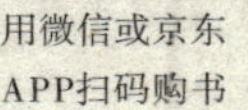

用微信或京东　　用淘宝APP
APP扫码购书　　扫码购书

3. 过绒管

左右手配合顺序过管挖花，将该铲次
应织的绒管分别引入后，纹刀抽出，
接着插入下一铲提起的花经开口中。

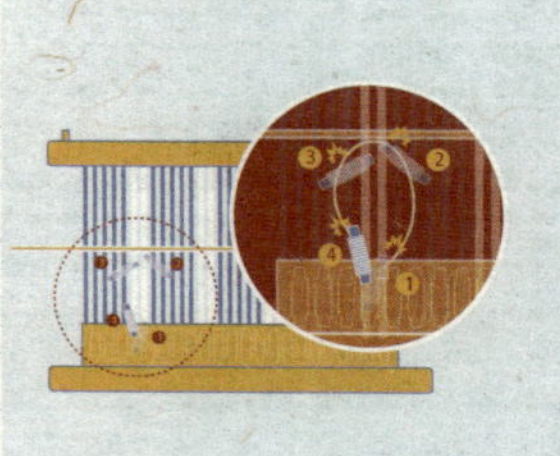

4. 抛梭

经丝形成开口后，用梭子在经丝开口内往
返，抛梭将纬丝引入。

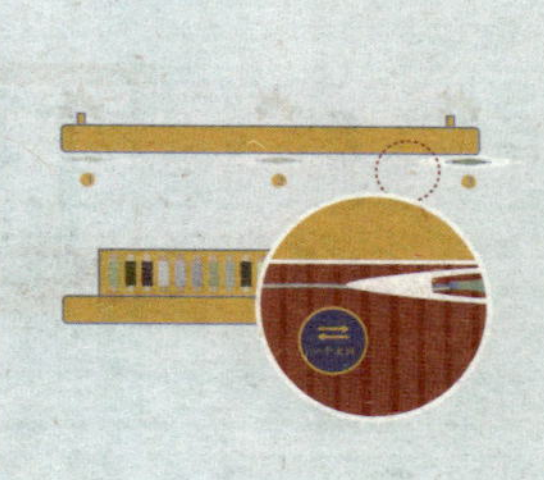

5. 打纬

俗称"碰框"。打纬时，左脚脱离脚竹，
踩踏马竹，高压板回升脱剎，然后用
双手扶住框盖将𥫱框拉向织口，把纬
丝打紧。

版权　南京江南丝绸文化博物馆　南京艺术学院

作者　王珂滢　杨章彬　钱佰慧

指导老师　师　悦

5·织造步骤

　　织花工手主要进行抛梭、铲纹刀、过绒管、打纬等作业，脚主要进行踏脚竹带动范幛开口和制动筘框等作业。操作是协同连贯的，有基本的程序、规律，但也要随着纹样的变化不断进行调整。

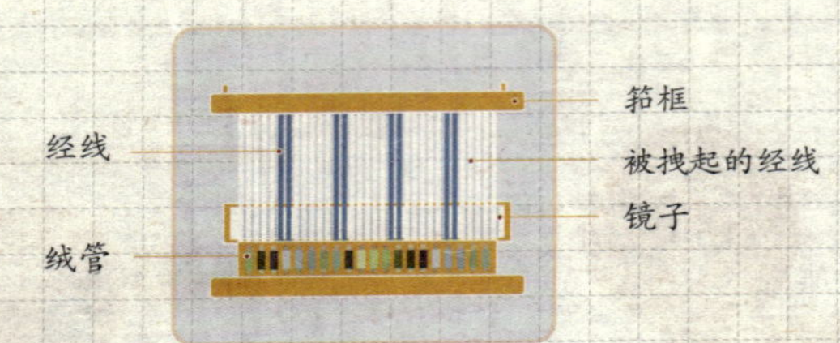

1. 形成梭口

织花工脚踩踏脚竹，使经线形成大面积梭口。

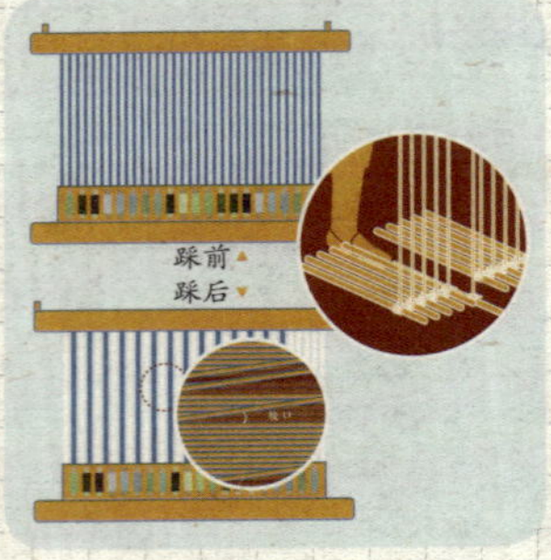

2. 铲纹刀

当拽花工提起经丝形成开口后，织花工将纹刀插入并翻转 90 度，使纹刀撑开梭口上下层经丝。

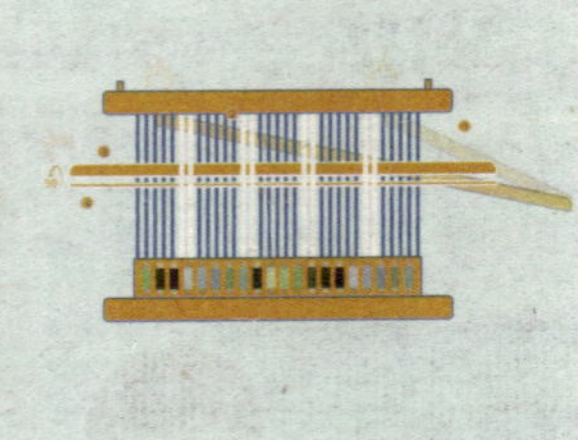

4·织机装造

根据所织云锦的品种、规格，把织造云锦所需的经丝，按地部组织、纹部组织的不同要求分别安装到位，使其符合织造的需要。

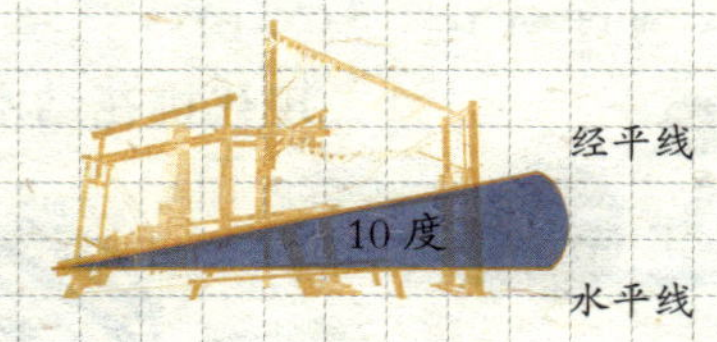

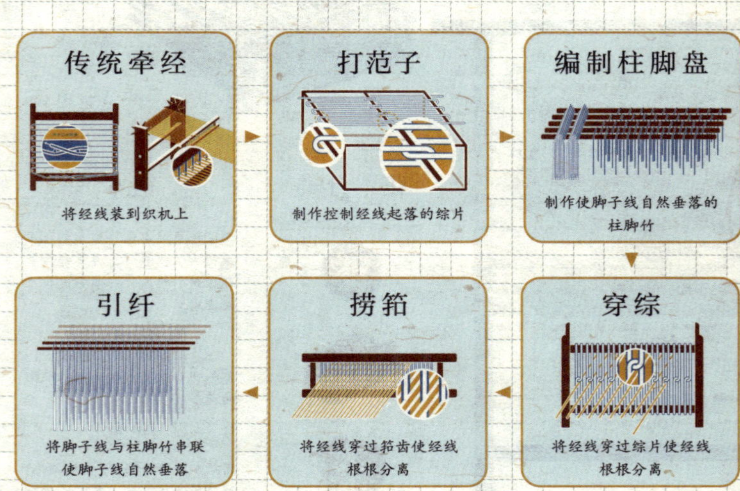

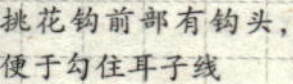

现代挑花结本方式

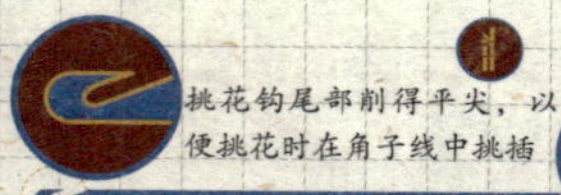

花本分类

祖本

通过挑花结本制作出来的花本被称为"祖本"，通常作为长期保存的样本，一般不直接上机使用。

行本

把从祖本上复制出来上机使用的花本叫"行本"。

拼本

用挑制的局部花本，经过倒花、拼花等多次复制工艺，最后制成完整的花本，叫"拼本"。

3·挑花结本

　　挑花结本，是中国古代丝织提花生产上的一项关键工艺和重要环节。传统的挑花方法，是在图案纸样上画若干方格，分成若干区，计算好每一区的经纬线数，全凭挑花艺人的丰富经验随画量度，算计分寸，用一竹片钩子，挑起脚子线，引入耳子线，编结而成。

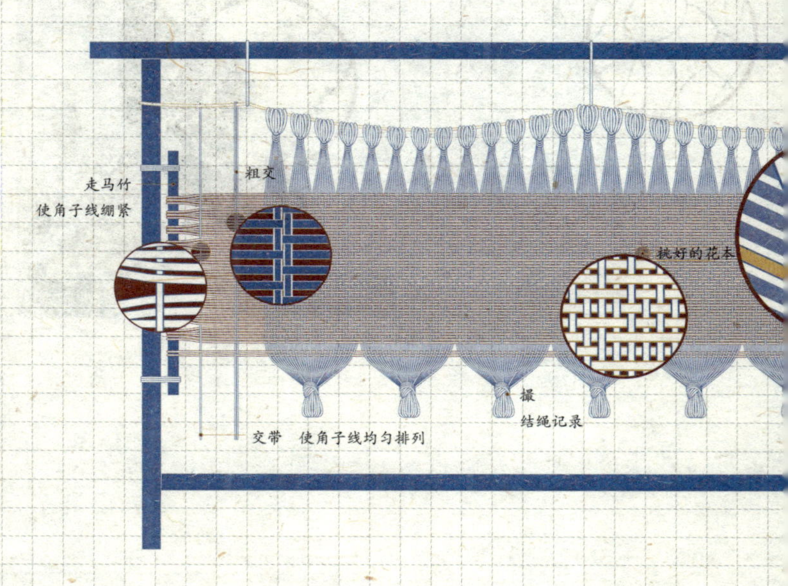

纬线数：长度 ＝ 纬密　经线数：宽度 ＝ 经密

2 · 设计意匠

纹样设计即创作云锦纹样图案。当设计人员将纹样、组织、规格等设计好之后，根据设计填绘意匠图。意匠纸是特制的，上面有纵横小格，小格的纵横比例代表织物经纬线密度。

1 准备纸墨笔，想出样式

2 设计样式，画出线稿

3 设计颜色，绘制彩稿及意匠稿

古代横顺格打法   现代电脑输出

1. 用尺按寸定线位

2. 将纸对折用狼毫笔蘸墨轻抹侧边

3. 成格后轻抹侧边横竖线交叉处用笔尖点上黑点为寸格记号

4. 将寸格对折再对折抹上黑线称"分四牙"

5. 随着现代科技的发展，通过电脑绘制、打印等技术，制作格子纸变得简单便利

织造流程

1·材料准备

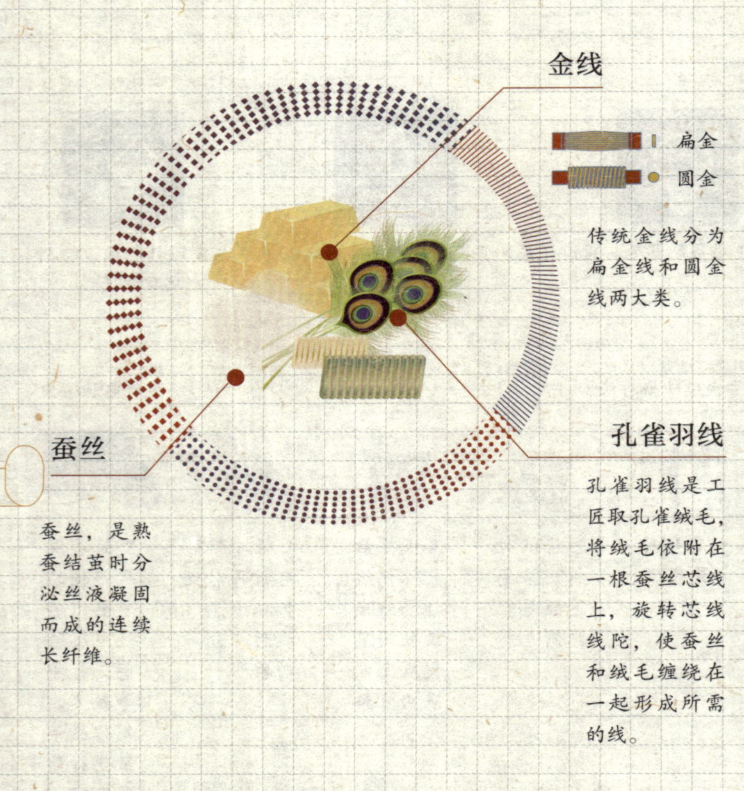

金线

传统金线分为扁金线和圆金线两大类。

蚕丝

蚕丝，是熟蚕结茧时分泌丝液凝固而成的连续长纤维。

孔雀羽线

孔雀羽线是工匠取孔雀绒毛，将绒毛依附在一根蚕丝芯线上，旋转芯线线陀，使蚕丝和绒毛缠绕在一起形成所需的线。

Contents